THE WORLD OF SCIENCE
HOW EVERYDAY THINGS WORK

THE WORLD OF SCIENCE
HOW EVERYDAY THINGS WORK

CHRIS COOPER
& TONY OSMAN

Facts On File Publications
New York, New York ● Bicester, England

HOW EVERYDAY THINGS WORK

Copyright © Orbis Publishing Limited 1984
Copyright © Macdonald & Co (Publisher) Ltd 1988

First published in the United States of America in
1984 by Facts on File, Inc., 460 Park Avenue South,
New York, N.Y. 10016

First published in Great Britain in 1984 by Orbis
Publishing Limited, London

**Library of Congress Cataloging in Publication
Data**

Main entry under title:

The world of science.

Includes index.
Summary: A twenty-five volume encyclopedia of
scientific subjects, designed for eight- to twelve-year-
olds. One volume is entirely devoted to projects.
1. Science—Dictionaries, Juvenile.   1. Science—
Dictionaries
Q121.J86   1984   500   84-1654

ISBN: 0-87196-988-2

Printed in Italy
10 9 8 7 6 5 4 3

Jacket photo courtesy of
Joel Gordon/Copyright © 1983

Previous pages Today's
BMX bicycles are a
great contrast to the
high-wheelers or
penny-farthings (page
7) which were popular
about 100 years ago.

Consultant editors
Eleanor Felder, former managing editor, *New Book of
Knowledge*
James Neujahr, Dean of the School of Education, City
College of New York
Ethan Signer, Professor of Biology, Massachusetts
Institute of Technolgy
J. Tuzo Wilson, Director General, Ontario Science
Centre

Editor Penny Clarke
Designer Roger Kohn

CONTENTS

Note There are some unusual words in this book. They are explained in the Glossary on pages 62 and 63. The first time each word is used in the text it is printed in *italics*.

▶Charlie Chaplin is probably one of the most famous of all film stars. Most of his best-known films were silent, but that has not lessened their popularity over 50 years later. Here he is in *The Gold Rush*.

1 FORCES AND MOVEMENT AT WORK

CYCLES

It has taken over a hundred years to develop the bicycle to its modern form. The bicycle is now very light and comfortable to ride, but it was not like that when it first appeared in the 19th century.

The first bicycle to be made and sold in large numbers was invented by two Frenchmen, Pierre Michaux and his son Ernest, who lived in Paris. They put pedals on the front wheel of their bicycle, like the pedals on the front wheel of the tricycles that very young children still ride today. They called their new machine a 'velocipede', and it was much lighter and more comfortable than any previous design for a bicycle. But the rider had to pedal very quickly to keep going, even so the velocipede was popular, and by 1865 they were making 400 a year.

To avoid this, and so make things easier for the rider, the front wheels of later bicycles were made much larger

▼Velocipedes were popular in the 1860s. Notice the position of the saddle and how the pedals are part of the front wheel.

than the back wheels. Each time the rider turned the pedals once, the front wheel turned once – so the larger the front wheel was, the farther the bicycle

▲In the early days of cycling some very odd looking machines were produced. The manuped was driven by the driver using his hands to push levers.

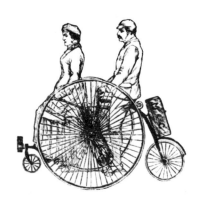

▲A tricycle for two with a fourth wheel. The wheel at the front was a safety measure to stop the machine tipping over if the brakes were put on suddenly.

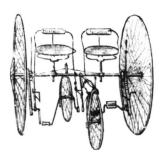

▲Riders sat beside each other on this aptly named 'Sociable' quadricycle. Pedals and cranks drove the two large wheels by chains.

▲The 'Invincible', another tricycle built for two, but this one does not have a safety wheel. It was driven by pedals and cranks and chains to the back wheels.

6

would travel in that turn. So the rider could pedal quite slowly, yet the bicycle would move fast.

Soon the front wheels of bicycles were made very large – as much as 1½ m (5 ft) across, while the rear wheel was very small. Bicycles like this were difficult to ride, with their thin tyres of solid rubber and saddles so high that you could not put a foot on the ground when you stopped. And they could be dangerous, because the rider was placed so far forward that if the bicycle hit a large bump he would fall over the handlebars.

The 'Safety' bicycle

These faults were overcome in the 'Safety' bicycle. The first models were made in 1878. By 1885 they looked very much like a modern bicycle. It had two wheels of similar size, and the pedals turned the back wheels by means of a chain.

The chain was a very important invention. It runs around a large cogwheel, called a chainwheel, attached to the pedals, and around a smaller one, the sprocket, on the hub (the centre) of the rear wheel. Every time the cyclist turns the pedals once, the chainwheel turns once and the rear wheel turns several times – which is what the rider wants. A simple example shows how this works. Suppose the chainwheel has 48 teeth and the rear sprocket has 16 teeth. When the chainwheel turns once, it pulls round 48 links on the chain. And the chain forces the rear sprocket to turn three times (because 48 ÷ 16 is 3).

Bicycle gears

The Safety bicycle very quickly became more and more like the bicycles we now ride. One important invention was a way of changing gears. When you are cycling uphill, you change to a 'low' gear. This means that you do not have to push so hard. One way of doing this is to put several sprockets on the rear wheel – five is a common number nowadays. A lever moves the chain from one sprocket to another.

This type of gear is called a 'derailleur'. It has a spring system to take up the slack in the chain when you change from a larger to a smaller sprocket. Some

◄High-wheelers (penny-farthings) could be quite dangerous. Road surfaces were not as smooth as they are today and if the front wheel hit a stone or went into a rut, the rider was thrown over the handlebars.

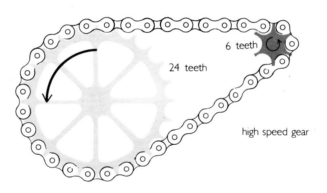

24 teeth   6 teeth
high speed gear

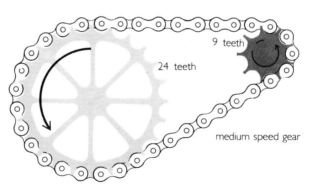

24 teeth   9 teeth
medium speed gear

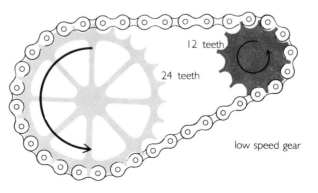

24 teeth   12 teeth
low speed gear

◄How the gears of a bicycle work. The larger chainwheel is the driver. The smaller ones (the sprockets) are fixed to the rear wheel and are driven. One turn of the chainwheel gives four turns of the rear wheel in top gear, three turns in mid gear and only two turns in low gear. Therefore the low gear is helpful when climbing hills, whereas high gear is best on level ground.

7

◀Racing bicycles such as this one have toe-clips on the pedals so the rider can pull on the up-stroke of the pedal as well as push on the down-stroke.

bicycles have two or more chainwheels, as well as several sprockets on the rear wheel, so the rider can choose from a very large number of gears.

Another kind of gear is called a 'hub gear'. The rear wheel has a large hub containing a rather complicated set of epicyclic gears. The rider usually has a choice of three, four or five gears.

◀A racing tandem built on the same principles as the bicycle above. It will, of course, be heavier because it must support the weight of two cyclists.

Tyres

The first Safety bicycles had solid tyres, but in 1888 the Scottish inventor John Boyd Dunlop took out a patent on a bicycle tyre that could be pumped up with air. Air-filled tyres give a much more comfortable ride on bumpy roads.

Brakes

◀A modern track racing bicycle is designed for lightness. There are no brakes, gears or fenders (mudguards). The tyres are made from light materials and may weigh only 100 grams (3½ oz) each.

On modern bicycles there is a brake on each of the wheels. They are controlled by brake levers, one on each handle, which you squeeze when you want to apply the brake. A cable joins each lever to the brake itself. When you pull the brake lever, you make rubber pads on the brake grip the wheel rim and slow the bicycle down. If you feel these pads – called 'brake blocks' – after a ride, you will find that they are hot. This is because a moving bicycle and its rider have a lot of *energy*, and you have to take some of this away in order to slow down. The brake blocks do this by turning the energy of movement into heat.

◀Folding bicycles may not be as light or fast as the racing machines above, but they are a very practical form of bicycle when storage space is limited.

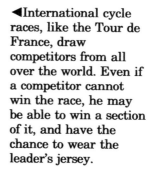

◀International cycle races, like the Tour de France, draw competitors from all over the world. Even if a competitor cannot win the race, he may be able to win a section of it, and have the chance to wear the leader's jersey.

▶Stunt bikes are a new development in the bicycle world. In contrast to the lightweight racing bicycles, they have to be tough and sturdy enough to withstand the jarring on landing.

GEARS

A gear is a wheel with teeth sticking out along its rim. The teeth can fit – 'mesh' – into the teeth of other gears and so turn them. They are used in all sorts of machinery, such as clocks, watches and bicycles. Trains, cars and planes use gears to turn the energy produced by burning fuel in their engines into movement of their wheels or propellers.

When you ride a bike you are using gears. A large gear fixed to the pedal drives a smaller gear at the rear wheel. Their teeth fit into a chain that runs around both gears. This chain not only meshes the gears, it allows them to turn in the same direction. If the gears were meshed directly together they would turn in opposite directions.

The pushing of your feet on the bike pedals is an example of what scientists call 'force'. Forces are simply pushes and pulls. A force is needed to start your bike moving. Your feet exert a force on the pedals, causing the chain to exert a force

▲A primitive type of gear system in use in an old mill near Baghdad, Iraq.

on the axle of the back wheel. When slowing down, the brakes press against the wheel rims, creating a force that slows the wheels.

Gears change the strength or direction of a force. The gears on a bike change the amount of force you need to exert. Riding a bike up a steep hill is harder than riding it on a level road, if you stay in the same gear. You can probably keep the bike moving, but you tire quickly. If you change to a lower gear, you find that you have to move your feet through a greater distance for each turn of the wheels. Because the feet are moving farther, they need not exert so much force to do a given amount of work. You have to move your feet faster to keep the bike going uphill; but less strength is needed, thanks to the work of gears.

◄Helical gears connect parallel shafts, as these would be, or shafts at an angle to each other but not meeting.

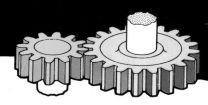

▲A spur gear. It is used when shafts (white) must rotate in the same plane. The teeth are straight and parallel to the shaft. The pinion (yellow) is the smaller of a gear pair.

▶An internal gear. The pinion rotates on the inside of a ring-type gear with straight teeth on its inner surface. This is a type of spur gear in which both the pinion and the gear turn in the same direction, unlike ordinary spur gears.

▶A helical gear. This has curved teeth at an angle to the shaft. These teeth grip with less noise than straight teeth, especially when they are turning at high speeds.

▶A herringbone gear. The teeth are V-shaped, like a double helical gear. The shafts rotate in opposite directions as in an ordinary spur gear.

▶A bevel gear. The teeth slope along one surface of the disc. The pinion rolls at an angle to the top of the gear, not along its edge. This type of gear is used when the shafts to be turned meet at an angle.

▼A planetary gear system. 'Planet' spur gears turn on a central 'sun' gear and an internal ring gear. This system is used in 'automatic' cars.

◀A worm gear. A screw pinion (the worm) turns along a spur gear. Motion can be transmitted between shafts that are at right angles.

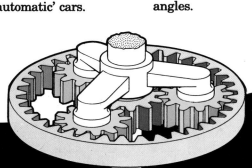

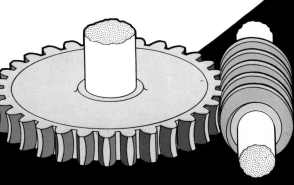

TYRES

Tyres are round coverings, made mostly of rubber. They are used to cover the rolling surfaces of wheels. Their material is much softer than the metal of which wheels are usually made. When a wheel rolls over a bump, its tyre can soften the impact.

A tyre also gives a wheel better contact with the road it is rolling on. Its softer material can 'grip' the road surface. So the wheel will move only by rolling, not by sliding. The vehicle will 'skid' less easily, even if the road is slippery with water or ice. Tyres serve as protection too. They prevent wheels from being worn down and from wearing away roads, by constant rolling.

Tyres are used on many vehicles. These include motor cars, bicycles, and aircraft. Tyres are of several types and sizes. A large earth-moving vehicle may have tyres 3 m (10 ft) in diameter. A small machine such as a vacuum cleaner has tiny tyres.

Early tyres

Solid rubber tyres were used on some early motor cars. But they had little 'give' and were hard on the road surfaces. They are now used only on some trucks and tractors. The 'pneumatic' tyre is the most common kind today. Its name means that it is filled with air. The air makes the tyre softer and more elastic than solid rubber.

Pneumatic tyres

A pneumatic tyre has an outer casing of strong rubber. This may contain a hollow inner tube of softer rubber. The tube holds the air, which is pumped into it. A pump is connected to the tube through the 'valve' which goes through the outer casing.

Such a tyre will lose its air if a hole is made in the tube. This may happen when a sharp object, such as a nail, breaks through the outer casing and punctures the tube. A 'tubeless' tyre is harder to puncture. In a tubeless tyre, the outer covering alone holds the air. The inner surface is sealed with a soft kind of rubber. Tubeless tyres are now used on most cars.

The outer surface of a tyre casing is not smooth. Its rubber is cut into a pattern of grooves. This 'tread' helps the tyre to grip the road. The rubber is also made stronger by 'vulcanisation'. It is heated together with sulphur. Then other chemicals such as carbon and zinc oxide are added to it.

A tyre casing is made even stronger by its construction. It has a 'skeleton' of metal and cloth. There are two hoops of steel that hold the tyre in place on the wheel. Several layers of fabric, such as cotton or nylon, form the outer surface. The layers have been dipped into hot liquid rubber. They are called the plies. But the side walls of the tyre are made of a soft rubber. Thus the walls can stretch as the tyre is inflated.

▼Diagrams showing how radial ply (**a**) and cross ply (**b**) tyres are constructed.

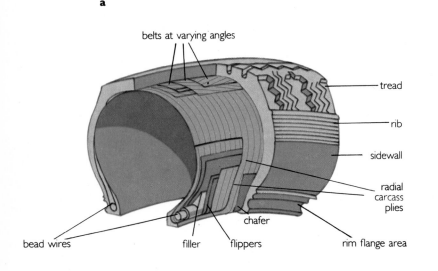

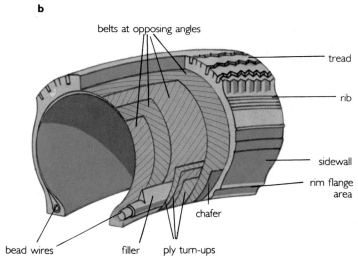

▼A 'burnout' at the start of a drag race. Bleach is poured under the tyres and the driver of the car spins his wheels. This makes the tyres' surface warm and sticky, increasing the friction with the track surface. It enables the car to get off to a good start. Once the car is moving, the tyres get warm and friction increases anyway.

►This wheel has a worn tyre, making it skim or 'hydroplane', over the wet road. It does not grip the surface and rotate. The water forced under the wheel cannot escape through the grooves in the threads, because these have been worn smooth. Instead, the water forces the wheel off the road surface.

KEITH BLACK
SIMPSON
HAYS

PUMPS

One of the simplest types of pump, and the one you will come across most frequently, is the one that you use to blow up the tyres on your bicycle. There is a long rod attached to the handle of the bicycle pump. At the end of the rod, inside the barrel of the pump, is a rubber cup or a disc of leather. When the pump handle is pushed down the air in the barrel is compressed, or squeezed, and its pressure (the force with which it tries to expand back again) increases. The pressure forces the edges of the rubber cup against the sides of the barrel, making it airtight. As you continue to push the handle, you increase the pressure inside the pump and air forces its way past the valve on your bicycle tyre and into the tyre. The valve lets air go only one way – into the tyre, but not out.

As you pull the pump handle out, the air pressure inside the pump gets less and less. It quickly becomes less than the pressure of the air outside the pump, and then air forces its way past the rubber cup and into the barrel. (The rubber cup acts as a valve, allowing air to flow into the pump, but not out.) When you push the handle in again, you drive this air into the tyre.

Pumps for lifting

The lift pump is also very easy to understand. As its name suggests, it is used to lift liquids – usually water. This is how a lift pump raises water from a well. There is a one-way valve on the piston, the piece of metal that moves up and down in the barrel of the pump. At the bottom of the pump is another valve. A tube goes from the bottom of the pump to the water in the well. When you use the pump, you raise the piston by pulling a lever upwards. As the piston rises, the space beneath it in the barrel of the pump increases, and the air pressure inside the pump decreases. The valve on the piston closes, preventing air from entering the barrel. At the bottom of the pump, the pressure of the atmosphere pushes water into the pump, past the lower valve.

When the piston is pushed downwards, the valve on the piston opens, while the valve at the bottom is forced shut by the pressure. So the piston moves down past the water in the barrel. When the piston is raised again, the valve on it closes. The piston lifts the water that is above it, and the water runs out of a tube in the side of the pump. At the same time, more water enters the pump beneath the piston, and the cycle is repeated.

The water is pushed into the pump by the pressure of the atmosphere on the water in the well. This pressure is strong enough to push water up by about 10 m (33 ft). But most pumps leak a little, and so can raise water by only about 8 m (26 ft).

Force pumps

You can raise water from more than 8 m (24 ft) below ground with a 'force pump'. There are no valves in the piston of a force pump; instead, there are two valves at the bottom of the barrel. One valve lets water in; the pipe from this goes to the underground water. The other valve lets water pass outwards only; the pipe from this leads to the surface. When the piston is raised, water enters the barrel through the 'in' valve, just as it does with the lift pump. When the piston is pushed down, the pressure on the water in the barrel is increased, and the 'in' valve is forced shut. The water is driven through the 'out' valve and forced towards the surface. The harder the piston is pushed down, the higher the water can be raised.

Lift pumps and force pumps are not

►Windmills use energy from the wind to power pumps used to drain wet, low-lying land.

14

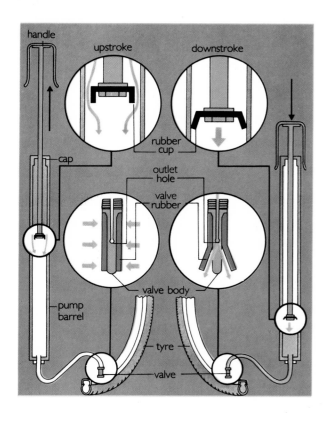

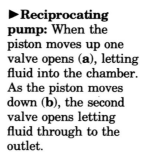

◄Diagram to show what happens inside a bicycle pump when it is used to pump air into bicycle tyres.

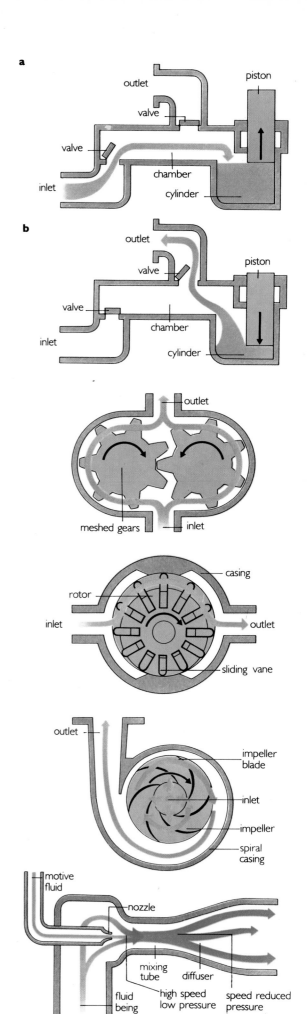

a

b

suitable for use with motors because the pistons have to be raised and lowered in a straight line. Motors are best used to provide power for circular motions. Gear pumps and centrifugal pumps work by a circular movement and are powered by engines.

Gear pumps

A gear pump contains two gear wheels that mesh, so that one drives the other. Each gear wheel is very deep from front to back, and has just a few very large teeth. When the pump is running, the water or other fluid is dragged through the pump by the teeth of the gear wheels, which act like paddles.

Centrifugal pumps

Inside a centrifugal pump there is a wheel, called an impeller. There are deep troughs cut into the impeller. As it turns the impeller scoops up a little of the liquid, carries it round and then throws it out of the pump by the force of the spinning. Other types of centrifugal pump have impellers that are shaped like the propeller of a ship, or the blades inside an aircraft's jet engine. As the impeller spins, the fluid is drawn in along the length of the impeller, and thrown out either behind it or from the side.

►**Reciprocating pump:** When the piston moves up one valve opens (**a**), letting fluid into the chamber. As the piston moves down (**b**), the second valve opens letting fluid through to the outlet.

►**Gear pump:** As the gears turn, fluid caught between their teeth is carried from the inlet to the outlet.

►**Vane pump:** Vanes slide out of the rotor at the inlet, carry fluid to the outlet and slide in again.

►**Centrifugal pump:** As the impeller rotates, the fluid is thrown outward from the central inlet through the blades to the spiral casing.

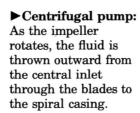

►**Jet pump:** As it goes through the nozzle, the jet of motive fluid (which may even be air) creates a low pressure. This draws the fluid to be pumped into the mixing tube.

ELEVATORS AND ESCALATORS

The invention of the lift, or elevator as it is known in the USA, made the skyscrapers of our city centres possible. Without it we should be limited to buildings that were only three or four storeys high.

An elevator is supported by a steel cable that runs from the top of the passenger cabin, over a large pulley wheel and down to a heavy weight that moves in a track at the back of the lift shaft. The 'counterweight' balances the weight of the elevator, so that less electric power is needed to move it. You can sometimes see the counterweight moving past while you wait for the elevator.

The elevator is moved by a powerful electric motor that drives the pulley wheel at the top of the shaft. It is controlled by buttons inside the cabin and also by others on each floor, by the doors.

Elevators are very safe. There are automatic brakes that lock the pulley wheel if the power supply fails. Automatic locks ensure that the elevator cannot move while the doors are open. The most important safety device is a set of claws fixed to the elevator itself. If the cable were to break, these would grab the tracks that the elevator runs in, and stop it from crashing to the ground.

Waiting for an elevator wastes time. So engineers have invented a 'continuous elevator'. There are two shafts, side by side. A number of elevators are attached to a cable and they move up one shaft, across to the other shaft at the top, and then come down. Each elevator is open at the front and they move slowly, so passengers step into one as it goes past and step out at the floor they want. If they make a mistake and do not get out at the right floor it does not matter, because the elevator stays the right way up as it crosses from one shaft to the other.

Escalators

An escalator is a moving staircase, that can move large numbers of people quickly without any waiting. The steps are separate from each other, but are joined to long belts that are driven by machinery. As the steps reach the top or bottom of the staircase, they flatten out. In between they stand out to make firm stairs that you can walk up or down while they move. There is also a moving handrail alongside, that is a continuous belt driven by the same motor. There are emergency buttons by the escalator so that it can be stopped instantly if there is an accident.

▼Moving paths without separate steps are often called travelators. They work in a similar way to escalators. Travelators are very useful in places like airports, where large numbers of people often have long distances to walk from the aircraft to passport control and the main airport building.

◀An escalator consists of a series of separate steps held in line by two chains rather like very heavy-duty bicycle chains. The chains are driven by large gear wheels at the top and bottom of the escalator, and this moves the steps in a continuous belt. Each step also has a pair of rollers to keep the step level.

motor

handrail drive chain

step

handrail

drive gear

rollers

roller guide rail

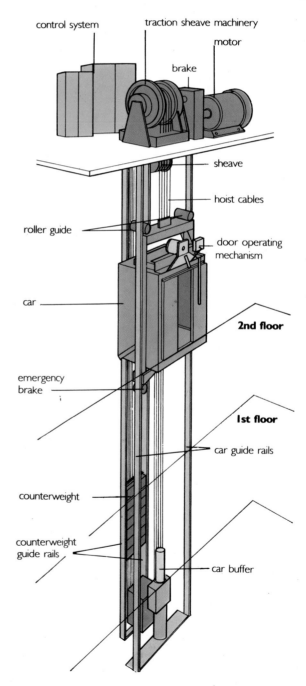

▲A modern elevator in the new headquarters of an international bank. The glass sided cars have been made a feature of the building, a great contrast to the more usual type of elevator tucked away behind heavy metal gates.

▶Most elevators are driven by electric motors. The sheave system includes a counterweight to balance the weight of the lift car. This takes some of the strain off the driving motor.

control system

traction sheave machinery

motor

brake

sheave

hoist cables

roller guide

door operating mechanism

car

2nd floor

emergency brake

1st floor

car guide rails

counterweight

counterweight guide rails

car buffer

SCREWS

Screws are valuable in woodworking because they can hold two pieces of wood together very securely. In engineering they are essential for joining pieces of metal together.

The most important part of the screw is its 'thread' – the raised spiral that runs along it. A screw that is to be used in wood has a pointed end and is tapered. The thread is sharp so as to cut into the wood. There is a slot – a groove – cut across the head of the screw, so that it can be turned with a screwdriver. There is always a risk that the screw will split the wood as it is driven in. The risk can be reduced if a small hole is drilled at the place where the screw is to be used.

Engineers sometimes use screws very similar to wood screws for fastening pieces of metal together. These must be tougher than woodscrews, but they are used in the same way. The head of this kind of screw may have a slot in the form of a cross. A screwdriver with a cross-shaped tip is used to drive the screw in with great force.

Bolts

A bolt is often used to hold pieces of metal together. A bolt is a screw that does not taper. After passing through the hole, it usually goes through a nut – a small piece of metal with a hole through it. The inside of the hole in the nut has a thread, which grips the thread on the screw tightly. The threads on the bolt and the nut must match exactly. The nut and bolt are tightened with a spanner and make a very secure join.

Screw-jacks

The idea behind the screw can be used for quite different purposes. The screw-jack that is used to lift cars is an example. One type of screw-jack consists of a very large screw with a metal plate at one end. The screw is placed underneath the car in an upright position, with the metal plate fitting under the bottom of the car. When the screw is turned, it is forced upwards, just as a woodscrew, when twisted, is forced through the wood. As the screw-jack rises, it lifts the car.

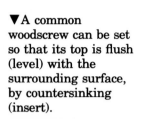

▼A common woodscrew can be set so that its top is flush (level) with the surrounding surface, by countersinking (insert).

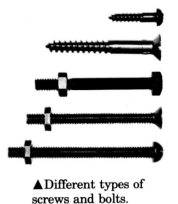

▲Different types of screws and bolts.

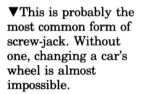

▲An expansion bolt. As the bolt is tightened, the wedge nut causes the anchor to expand and grip its surroundings.

▼This is probably the most common form of screw-jack. Without one, changing a car's wheel is almost impossible.

LOCKS AND KEYS

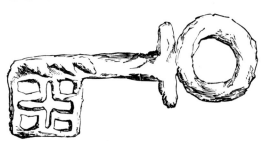

▲Ancient key found by archaeologists in the ancient Roman cities of Pompeii and Herculaneum in southern Italy. The cities were buried when Mt Vesuvius erupted in AD 79.

The lock that is most commonly used on outside doors today is the Yale lock, named after its American inventor, Linus Yale. In this lock, the bolt – the part that holds the door shut – has to be drawn back by using the key to turn a cylinder connected to the bolt. The cylinder can be turned by the correct key, but not by any other. As the key is turned in the lock, its jagged 'teeth' or drivers, raise a number of tiny bolts, called pins. If each pin is not raised to exactly the right height, the cylinder cannot turn. A key of the wrong shape will not raise the pins by the right amount.

A hotel manager often has a master key with which he can enter any room when necessary. All the Yale locks on the rooms are fitted with extra pins, which work only with the master key. Apart from the master key, only the room's own special key will open the lock.

But when you open the door from the inside, you do not have to use the key. You turn a knob that draws back the bolt directly.

Yale locks are not very strong. Many people fit a mortise lock as well, for extra security, and they are also used on doors inside the house. The bolt goes into a slot – called a mortise – cut into the door's wooden frame. The bolt is prevented from being drawn out of the mortise by several metal frames, called tumblers, inside the lock, which jam against a stud on the bolt. When a correctly shaped key is turned in the lock, its teeth lift the tumblers by just the right amount to form a slot through which the stud can pass. The same action of turning the key also draws the bolt.

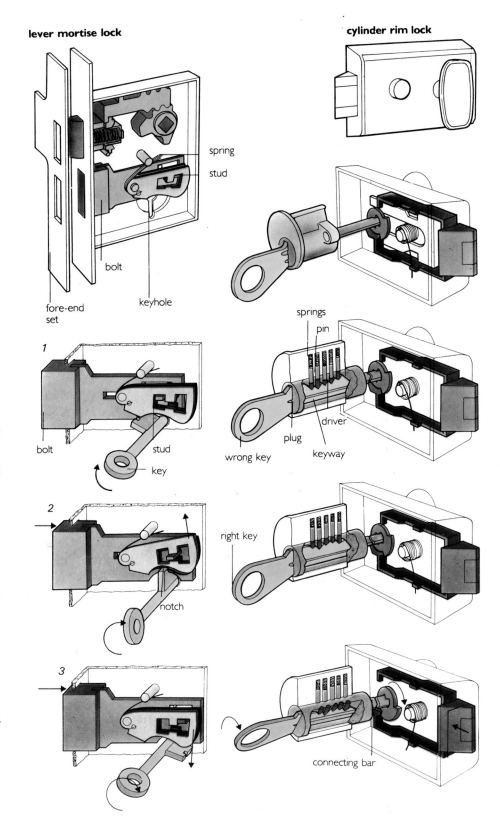

▲In the lever mortise lock the stud attached to the bolt prevents it being forced open when it is locked.
1 To unlock the bolt the lever tumblers (blue) must be lined up by the correct key, with the notch in the right place. When the tumblers are lined up, a gap or 'gate' is made through which the stud can pass.
2 Then the key can draw back the bolt.
3 When the bolt is unlocked, the action of the spring makes the tumblers fall back. The greater the number of tumblers, the more protection the lock gives.

▲The cylinder rim lock, commonly called the Yale lock after its inventor, is very hard to open without the right key. The pins and teeth, or drivers, must be lined up so the key will turn. The wrong key cannot do this.

19

TYPEWRITERS

▲This rare old typewriter was designed for typing musical scores. It certainly made the difficult and laborious task of preparing musical manuscripts for printing much easier, because without a typewriter it all had to be done by hand.

▲This Remington typewriter made in 1877 was one of the first really practical typewriters. One of the major problems to be overcome was that, when typing rapidly, the type bars carrying the different letters hit each other and became stuck. To overcome this problem, the Remington designers arranged the keyboard so that those letters that occurred most often together in words were separated from each other in the mechanism, though not necessarily on the keyboard. The arrangement of the lettered keys on this old typewriter is very similar to the arrangement on modern ones.

Many typewriters are still of the 'manual' type – that is, they are worked entirely by hand. The typist uses his or her fingers and hands to type the letters and move the paper. Electric and electronic typewriters use electricity to do most of the work.

When you press a key on a manual typewriter a lever connected to the key makes a piece of metal called a type bar fly over and hit the typewriter ribbon, pressing it briefly against the paper. The type bar has a raised surface in the shape of the letter that you want to type (though the letter is back to front, like a reflection in a mirror). The usual type of ribbon is made of cloth soaked in ink, and so the shape of the letter – the right way round – is printed on the paper. Pressing the key also moves the typewriter 'carriage', carrying the paper, one space to the left, and lifts the ribbon into position for the type bar. So the typist has to press hard. At the end of a line the typist pushes the carriage to the right and the paper is automatically moved upwards by one line.

One kind of electric typewriter uses much the same principle. But it has an electric motor to drive the type bar against the ribbon and to move the carriage. The typist does not have to press the keys hard and so can type much faster.

'Golf ball' typewriters
In the 'golfball' typewriter all the type is arranged around the surface of a ball. The ball moves along the paper as each line is typed. It turns around rapidly so that the right letter hits the ribbon as each key is pressed. A golfball typewriter is faster than an ordinary electric typewriter. It has a further advantage – you can change the kind of type you use simply by changing the golfball. So if you want to type something in italics (sloping letters) or in a different alphabet, such as the Greek or Russian alphabet, it is very easy to do so.

Electronic typewriters
Electronic typewriters use microchips to control the printing of the letters.

Pressing a key simply closes a switch underneath the keyboard, so that a small electric current tells the typewriter which letter is to be printed. Most electronic typewriters have a 'memory' – they will store a number of letters in a microchip before printing them out. They may store just a few letters, which are shown on an LCD display like the ones on calculators and digital watches. The letters on the screen can be changed by the typist if he or she makes a mistake or has a change of mind. As the typist continues working the new letters appear on the screen, while the old ones disappear from the screen as they are printed, one by one.

More advanced typewriters can store hundreds or thousands of words and print them out again and again at the press of a key. The typewriter can also be connected to a computer and a television screen, so that the text can be displayed on the screen and changed easily and quickly. It is printed out only when the typist is satisfied that it is exactly right. This kind of set-up is called a word processor.

You can type very fast on an electronic typewriter because the keys do not have to be moved very far – just far enough to close a switch. If the typewriter is connected to a computer, it will have to print words faster than any human being could type them. So new ways of printing the words, faster even than the golfball, have been invented. The daisy wheel or petal wheel typewriter has the letters at the end of springy rods arranged like the spokes of a wheel or the petals of a daisy. The 'wheel' spins very fast and a hammer strikes the 'spoke' as it goes past, to make the letters appear on the paper. The wheel moves from left to right across the paper.

Another kind of typewriter uses 'dot matrix' printing, in which each letter, number or other symbol is made up of tiny dots selected from a grid or 'matrix' of possible positions. Dot matrix printing can be difficult to read but is very fast. It is not often used on typewriters, but is more usual on printers connected directly to computers. Such printers often use daisy wheels, too.

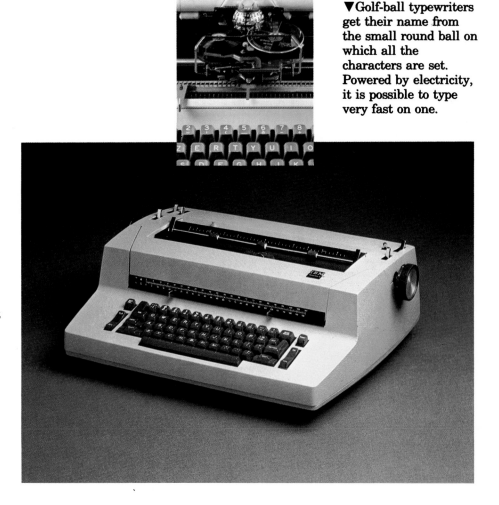

▼Golf-ball typewriters get their name from the small round ball on which all the characters are set. Powered by electricity, it is possible to type very fast on one.

▼Electronic typewriters are extremely sophisticated machines, most have 'memories', and many will link up to computers. But compare the keyboards of these three typewriters – they are all very similar.

SEWAGE WORKS

Sewage consists of the liquid and solid wastes that flow from lavatories and drains. It contains human waste, decaying food and other rotting materials. It must be purified so that it does not cause disease. Sewage works purify water so effectively that in many towns some of the drinking water has, at some point, been through a sewage works and yet is perfectly safe.

In the first stage of sewage treatment, wire nets are used to remove large pieces of solid matter. Then the liquid is allowed to run slowly through wide pipes, so that grit and small stones settle out. These two stages remove harmless rubbish.

Then the dangerous wastes – rotting material and wastes from lavatories – are allowed to settle out as sludge in large tanks. Sometimes the water from this tank is pumped into the sea or a fast-flowing river. The sewage water is mixed with such a large quantity of river or sea water that it is no longer a threat to health.

But sewage is often purified in a more thorough way. It is trickled through a tank that contains large stones. The stones are covered with a slime in which there are bacteria that can digest the

▲The inside of the Nashville Central Sewage Treatment Plant, Tennessee. Here, water containing industrial waste and domestic sewage is purified. Used water arrives at an underground chamber and is taken by pumps to where bacteria will continue the work of purifying it.

▼A sewage treatment plant, a familiar sight on the outskirts of most large towns and cities. This is the humus tank at one of many sewage works serving London.

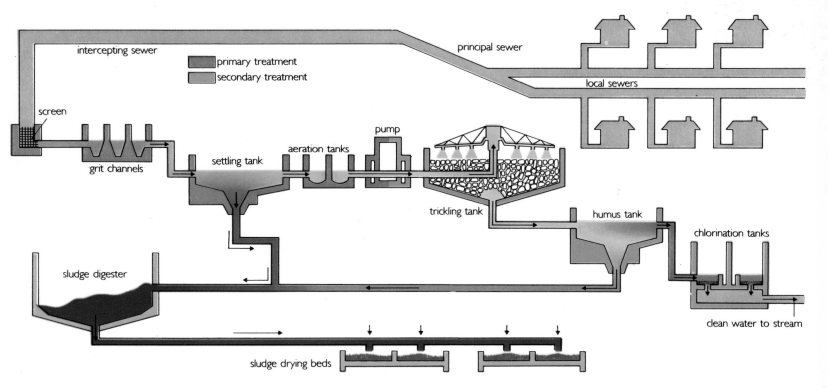

Labels in diagram: interecepting sewer, principal sewer, local sewers, primary treatment, secondary treatment, screen, grit channels, settling tank, aeration tanks, pump, trickling tank, humus tank, chlorination tanks, clean water to stream, sludge digester, sludge drying beds

▲This is how, in a very diagrammatic way, the sewage system in your town works.

▼Sometimes in country areas there may not be a main sewer or sewage disposal system as there is in a town. In such cases a house will have its own mini-sewage disposal system: a septic tank. Sewage flows into an underground tank. Solid matter settles at the bottom and is then broken up by bacteria. Liquid can overflow into another tank with bacteria. The liquid is purified and drains into the soil. The solid sludge has to be cleaned out of the tank at regular intervals.

dangerous substances in the sewage.

Then the water is pumped into settling tanks. Any remaining solids drift to the bottom of these tanks. Finally the water is purified with chlorine, a gas that kills bacteria. The water is now safe to drink and can be pumped into the local water supply. So some of the water you drink has already been drunk by other people – perhaps more than once.

The solid sludge must be disposed of. It is heated to make the purifying bacteria even more active. When it is quite safe it is sold to farmers as a fertilizer.

Knowing how we dispose of sewage may not seem nearly as interesting as, say, knowing how your transistor works, but safe disposed of sewage is utterly essential. Without it, life in large modern cities would be impossible, disease and vermin, such as rats, would see to that.

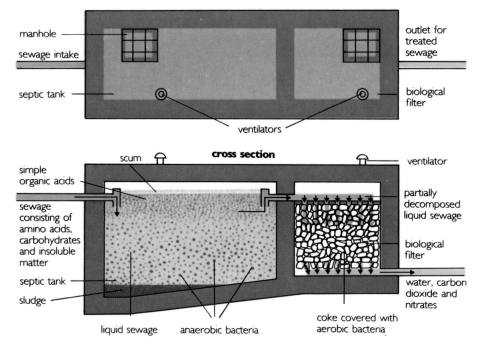

plan view of sewage treatment tank

Labels: manhole, sewage intake, septic tank, outlet for treated sewage, biological filter, ventilators

cross section

Labels: scum, simple organic acids, sewage consisting of amino acids, carbohydrates and insoluble matter, septic tank, sludge, liquid sewage, anaerobic bacteria, ventilator, partially decomposed liquid sewage, biological filter, water, carbon dioxide and nitrates, coke covered with aerobic bacteria

2

HEAT WORKS FOR US

AIR CONDITIONING

The air in a living room, an office or a factory should be cool and dry. This makes people more comfortable, and they can then relax more, or work better. In some factories it is also necessary to have extremely clean air, so that dust will not spoil the things that are being made.

Factories that make microchips for computers must have extremely clean air, because the tiniest speck of dust could spoil a microchip. Scientists have suggested that microchip factories could be set up in space, where there is no air at all.

Air conditioning is used a great deal in hot climates. But even in cooler countries it is valuable, because the air in a room or a building can become very hot if there

▲Air conditioning cools, dries and cleans air in homes or factories. In this electronics factory dust is constantly extracted by overhead suction pipes.

are a lot of people in it.

An air conditioning system works by blowing air over the cooling tubes of a refrigerator. If the air is moist, some of the water vapour that it contains will be lost – it will turn into liquid water and be left behind. This is because cool air cannot hold as much moisture as warm air can. The cool, dry air is then blown through filters that remove dust and smoke particles. These filters will also remove many of the smells that can make air unpleasant.

You will often find that the windows in air-conditioned buildings cannot be opened. This is to stop, hot, moist and dusty air entering from the outside.

The air in hot countries, or in crowded rooms and buildings in cool countries, is often very moist. Moist air makes a room unpleasant to be in. Because there is already so much water vapour in the air, the sweat on your skin cannot evaporate – that is, it cannot turn into water vapour, leaving your skin dry. And since the sweat cannot evaporate, it cannot carry heat away from your body and you cannot cool down. Air conditioning helps to keep you cool both by cooling the air and by removing the water vapour from it. The air conditioning system must also keep the air in a room moving. This keeps people more comfortable by helping the sweat on their skin to evaporate. The air conditioning system uses a fan to drive air into the room or factory.

Air conditioning is provided in some cars. Without it, the cars would be very uncomfortable to use in hot countries.

▼This diagram shows how air conditioning works. This equipment has a refrigeration unit in which gas circulates. The cold, liquified gas passes through a cooling coil and air is blown over the coil by the fan.

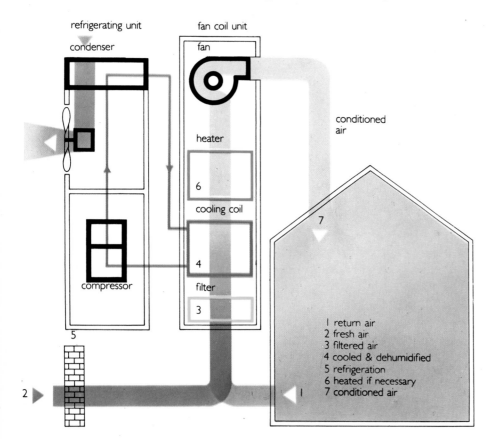

refrigerating unit

condenser

fan coil unit

fan

heater

6

cooling coil

conditioned air

4

compressor

filter

3

7

5

2 ▶

1 return air
2 fresh air
3 filtered air
4 cooled & dehumidified
5 refrigeration
6 heated if necessary
7 conditioned air

CENTRAL HEATING

In most central heating systems, water is heated in a boiler and then flows through pipes to radiators. The heat from the water in the radiators warms the room.

The water flows through the system because it expands when it is heated, and so becomes less dense. So the hot water rises and cold water moves down to replace it, causing the water in the whole system to circulate.

In the simplest central heating systems the water in the boiler is heated by burning coke, oil or gas. The hot water travels upwards from the boiler to the radiators, and the cold water in the system travels downwards through another set of pipes to the boiler. The hot water loses its heat while it passes through the radiators and is replaced by more hot water from the boiler.

The water is helped on its way by a pump. Most systems have a time switch that starts the boiler and the pump. The time switch is fully automatic, so the system can be switched on and off even when there is nobody available to operate it.

Central heating systems usually have a second set of pipes to take hot water from the boiler to a tank where it is stored. This part of the system has its own pump, so it can supply hot water for the kitchen and bathroom even in summer, when the radiators are not being heated.

Central heating using hot air

Some central heating systems use air, not water, to carry the heat. Hot air systems do not use radiators. The heated air flows into the rooms and warms them. This kind of central heating has a long history. The Romans heated their homes and public buildings with hot air circulating under the floors.

Steam heating

In some areas buildings are heated by steam from nearby power stations. The power stations produce the steam in order to generate electricity. Normally the steam is released into the air and the heat in it is wasted, but in this system the heat is put to good use. This

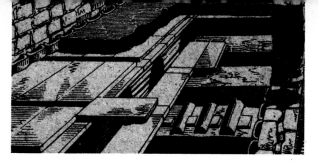

▲Archaeological drawing of the heating system built under the floor of the Roman villa excavated at Woodchester, in south-west England. Air heated by a furnace was circulated through a system of under-floor channels, so warming the rooms above.

technique is called 'district heating'. In New York City many of the skyscrapers are heated by steam that is produced specially for the purpose in central boilers and then carried to the buildings in underground pipes.

▼In a central heating system using hot water, the heated water is pumped along pipes to radiators in the rooms. The water in the boiler may be heated by gas, electricity, coal or oil, and regulated by a time-clock and thermostat. The expansion tank allows for overflow of water from the boiler. Radiators can be closed off in rooms where heat is not needed.

▼In a home heated by hot air, the air heated by the warm air unit is blown by fans along ducts to all the rooms. It goes through vents in the floors or walls into the rooms. Vents can be closed in rooms not used, or adjusted to control the amount of heat. Return air vents take the air back to the heater.

hot water

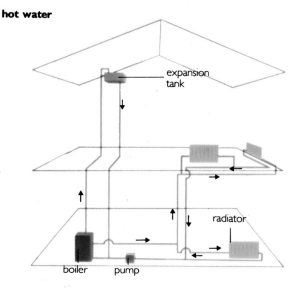

expansion tank

radiator

boiler   pump

warm air

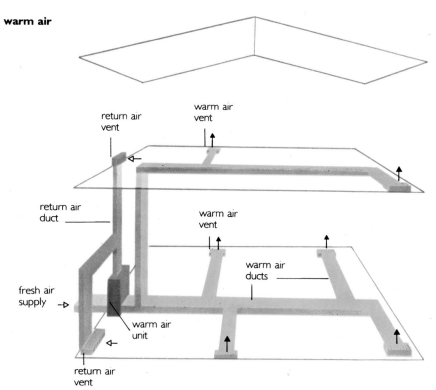

return air vent

warm air vent

return air duct

warm air vent

warm air ducts

fresh air supply

warm air unit

return air vent

REFRIGERATORS

A refrigerator's motor has to cool the space inside the refrigerator by taking heat from it. It gets rid of the heat into the air outside. Even when the refrigerator is cool, the motor has to continue working to remove heat that flows into the refrigerator from outside, through its walls.

Most home refrigerators work by turning a liquid, called a coolant, into a gas and then back into a liquid, over and over again. The coolant is usually a substance called Freon. The refrigerator's electric motor drives a pump that pushes the liquid coolant through a small hole into a long tube. This tube is usually at the top of the freezer compartment. The pump keeps the liquid at a high pressure to force it through the hole. Then, when the liquid has passed through the hole, it is no longer under high pressure and it evaporates – it turns into gas.

Whenever a liquid turns into a gas, it absorbs heat. (This is why your hands feel cold if they are damp. The moisture evaporates and absorbs heat from the hands.) So when the coolant turns into a gas, it absorbs heat from the freezer compartment of the refrigerator.

The gas travels on out of the freezer compartment and is compressed by the pump – squeezed under pressure so that it turns into a liquid. As it does so it gives out the heat that it absorbed previously. You can feel this heat coming from the tubes at the back of the refrigerator. Now the liquid is ready to be pumped round again.

▼A refrigerator on a very large scale – sides of beef hanging in a refrigerated warehouse. The coming of refrigeration made the transport of food much easier, and enabled Australia and New Zealand to build up their great industries exporting meat and dairy products, particularly to Europe.

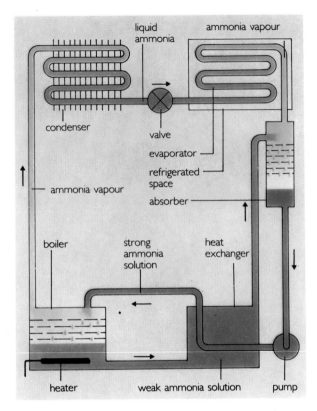

▲This is how an ordinary domestic refrigerator works.

Another type of refrigerator

Some refrigerators do not have motors and pumps. They are worked instead by a small electric heater or even by a gas flame. You may be surprised that a flame can be used to make things cool. This is how these refrigerators work. They contain a solution of ammonia – that is, water in which the gas ammonia has been dissolved. (You may have a bottle of strong-smelling liquid labelled 'ammonia' at home. This is actually a strong solution of ammonia in water.) When the ammonia solution in a refrigerator is heated, some of the ammonia is set free as gas and passes into the tube at the back of the refrigerator. As more and more gas is boiled off from the solution, the pressure rises in this tube. It rises so high that the gas turns into liquid ammonia, giving out heat as it does so. Then the liquid passes through a small hole into a tube in the freezer compartment and turns into gas, absorbing heat. The gas continues through tubes until it is dissolved in water again, and the cycle is repeated.

THERMOMETERS

Thermometers measure temperature – that is, how hot or cold something is. It can be the temperature of objects, of liquids or of the air in a room.

You might have seen the simplest type of thermometer hanging on the wall of a room. It consists of a sealed glass tube with a bulb – a wider part – at one end. The bulb is filled with a liquid, which comes part of the way up the tube. The liquid may be mercury, which is a silvery colour, or alcohol that has been coloured red.

Nearly all materials expand – get larger – when they are heated. Mercury and alcohol expand a great deal. The higher the temperature, the farther the liquid in a thermometer rises up the tube. You see which marking on the glass the liquid has reached, and this tells you the temperature.

There are two different ways of marking temperatures on a thermometer. One is called the Fahrenheit scale, after its inventor, Gabriel Fahrenheit, an 18th-century scientist. On this scale, the temperature at which water freezes – its freezing point – is 32 degrees. This is written as 32°F. The temperature at which water boils – its boiling point – is 212°F.

The other scale that you will see on a thermometer is called the centigrade or Celsius scale. Anders Celsius was an 18th-century Swedish scientist. 'Centigrade' means 'having a hundred steps'. On the centigrade scale, the freezing point of water is 0 degrees, written as 0°C. The boiling point is 100 degrees, or 100°C. You will often see the Fahrenheit scale marked along one side of a thermometer and the centigrade scale marked along the other.

A doctor uses a special kind of mercury thermometer. It is made so that when you take the thermometer out of your mouth, the mercury stays up in the tube – it does not immediately begin to fall back to show room temperature. This gives the doctor time to see what your temperature is. Afterwards he shakes the thermometer to force the mercury down. Another kind of thermometer, often used

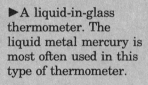

►A liquid-in-glass thermometer. The liquid metal mercury is most often used in this type of thermometer.

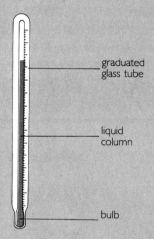

graduated glass tube

liquid column

bulb

◄Anders Celsius, the Swedish scientist who in 1742 described his centigrade scale of temperature. This temperature scale is now often called by his name, Celsius.

in greenhouses, has two little markers inside the tube. One is pushed upwards as the mercury rises, but is left behind when it falls. At the end of the day it shows the highest temperature reached. The other marker is pushed downwards when the mercury falls, and is left behind when it rises. So at the end of the night it shows the lowest temperature reached. This is important to a gardener, who wants to be sure that plants are not being damaged by too much heat or cold.

Alcohol boils at a much lower temperature than water, so an alcohol thermometer cannot be used to measure the temperature of water that is almost boiling. A mercury thermometer can be used up to about 300°C (570°F). But above that temperature the glass becomes soft and the mercury is close to boiling. Scientists and engineers have to use special kinds of thermometer to measure very high temperatures.

Different types of thermometer

One kind consists of two strips of different metals joined together along their length, and bent into a spiral. This is called a 'bimetallic strip' ('bi-' means 'two'). The outer end is fixed, while the inner end is connected to a pivot and a pointer. As the strip gets hotter, both metals will expand. But one will expand more than the other, so the bimetallic strip becomes more curved and the spiral coils up more tightly. As the strip cools, both metals contract, but again one metal will change size faster than the other. So now the bimetallic strip will straighten out a little, and the spiral will uncoil. These changes move the pointer around a scale. There may be one of these thermometers built into the door of the oven in your kitchen.

Another kind of thermometer is called a 'resistance' thermometer. It uses a battery, a coil of special wire, and an instrument that measures how much electric current is flowing through the wire. The higher the temperature, the higher the wire's electrical resistance – that is, the less current it allows to flow. So measuring the current shows what the temperature is.

Yet another kind of thermometer uses a 'thermocouple'. This consists of a metal wire joined at each end to another wire made of a different metal. The two joins are called 'junctions'. One junction is kept ice-cold. The other is put into the place where you want to measure the temperature. Because the two junctions are at different temperatures, the wires become a weak electric battery. The hotter the hot junction becomes, the higher the voltage that is generated. So this can be measured with a voltmeter that has its dial marked with degrees centigrade or Fahrenheit instead of volts.

◀Taking a patient's temperature with a thermometer is one of the quickest and most reliable ways for a doctor to find out if someone is ill.

▶Many industries rely on thermometers. Without a thermometer it is difficult to tell accurately if a furnace is the right temperature. Modern industries require absolute accuracy.

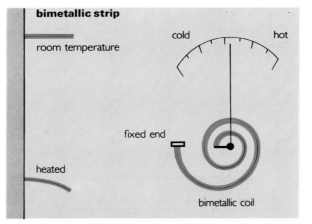

◀A bimetallic strip thermometer of the kind often used in thermostats. The movement of the bimetallic strip can be used to control the thermostat switching mechanism.

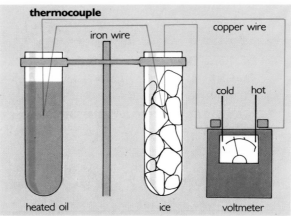

◀The thermocouple thermometer is useful for measuring very high temperatures.

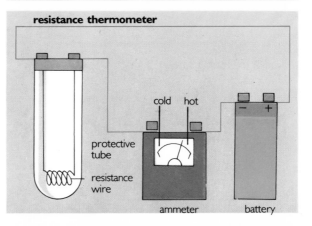

◀The resistance thermometer is the most accurate up to about 600°C (1112°F). It is widely used in science and industry, where temperatures of this magnitude need to be measured.

CAMERAS AND FILM

▼The parts of a single-lens reflex camera and how it works. The lens system focuses light from the image onto the film. The shutter is a metal blade in front of the film that moves away to let light reach the film. How much light enters the lens is controlled by the iris. Cameras like this can take very sharp pictures because of the accurate focusing allowed by the viewing system – the photographer sees the image that he is going to photograph through the lens that forms it. The small drawing shows the path the light takes through the camera. The mirror projects the image onto the Fresnel screen. Then the image is turned right way up by the pentaprism. The eyepiece, or viewfinder,

magnifies the image and makes it brighter so that it can be clearly viewed by the photographer. The mirror flicks out of the way as the shutter is released and the picture taken. The pressure plate keeps the film flat so that the image remains in focus over all the film.

Basically a camera is just a box with a lens at the front and film at the back. Light cannot get into the camera until you actually take a picture. Then a shutter opens briefly, allowing light that has come through the lens to fall on the film. In some cameras the shutter looks like a small roller blind, just in front of the film. Another type of shutter is placed just behind the lens.

The film needs just the right amount of light to make a good picture. One way of controlling the amount of light that reaches the film is by varying the

exposure time – that is, the length of time for which the shutter is open. The exposure time can be varied with a control on the camera. The control is marked with times that may range from a thousandth of a second to half a second. It is also possible to set the shutter so that it will stay open for as long as the shutter button is pressed, or until it is pressed for a second time. These very long times are used when the scene being photographed is very dark.

Another way of controlling the amount of light reaching the film is by varying the 'aperture'. There is a shield behind the lens, called the iris. There is a hole in the iris that can be made bigger or smaller. The size of the hole is called the aperture. On the camera's aperture control there is a series of numbers. Some of these numbers are 4, 5.6, 8, 11. The bigger the number, the smaller the aperture, and so the less light that can

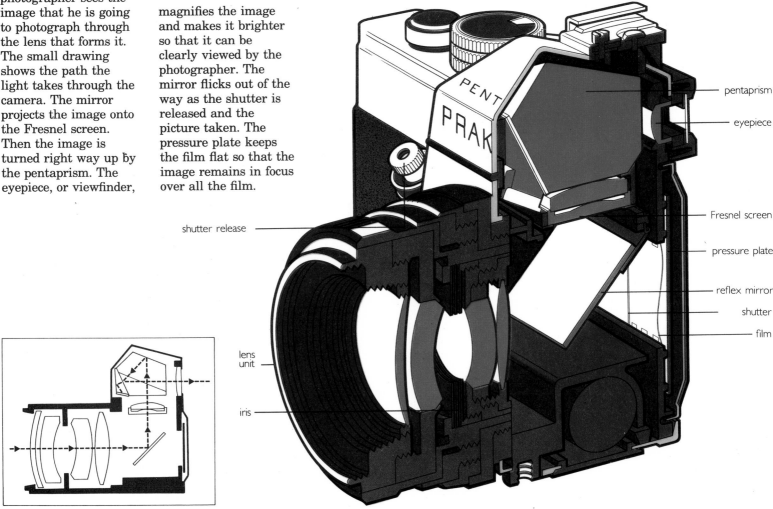

shutter release

lens unit

iris

pentaprism

eyepiece

Fresnel screen

pressure plate

reflex mirror

shutter

film

◀Different focusing gives different results. The chess board was photographed with the camera at maximum aperture and the effect was out of focus. However, when the lens only has a small aperture the entire board is in focus.

get through the iris. If you turn the aperture control from one setting to the next larger one – say, from 8 to 11 – the amount of light that can get through is cut by a half.

Photographers choose the exposure time and aperture that are best for the particular picture they are taking. If they are photographing someone running, for example, they will use a short exposure time to reduce the amount of blurring caused by the runner's movement. They choose a larger aperture to compensate for the short exposure time and so make sure the film gets enough light.

Many cameras have 'automatic exposure control'. A device called a *photo-electric cell* built into the camera measures the amount of light coming from the scene and sets the right aperture, and perhaps the exposure time as well.

Focusing the image

The camera must also be 'focused' correctly. The photographer turns the ring in which the lens is mounted, and the lens moves backwards or forwards, closer to or farther from the film. This is because the lens forms sharp images – pictures – of objects at different places according to how far away the objects are. A sharp image of a distant object is formed a short distance behind the lens, so the lens needs to be close to the film. A sharp image of a nearby object is formed farther from the lens, so the lens needs to be farther from the film. (See lenses, page 33.)

In some very simple cameras, however, the lens cannot be moved. In the pictures they produce, the closest and farthest objects are not in very sharp focus. So the photographer has to make sure that he or she takes pictures only of people or things at in-between distances – family groups, for example.

Some cameras can now focus automatically. One sort uses a pulse of 'ultrasonic' sound. This is sound of such a high *frequency* – high pitch – that human beings cannot hear it. When the photographer presses a button, the camera sends out the pulse. A detector on the camera can 'hear' an echo caused by

the sound reflected from the person or object being photographed. The camera measures the time delay between sending out the pulse and 'hearing' the echo. This tells it how far away that person or object is, because the sound travels at a known speed. A motor in the camera then moves the lens to the right position to give a sharply focused picture.

Another type of self-focusing camera does not use sound. A built-in computer examines the image formed by the lens. It adjusts the lens position until the image is sharply focused, and then takes the picture.

▼Photographs can be taken underwater by using cameras specially made to withstand the pressure of the water. Water filters some colours out of sunlight and below 15m (50ft) only blue and green are visible. Powerful artificial lights then have to be used to take pictures of undersea plants and animals in their real colours.

Viewfinders and eyepieces

The camera must have a viewfinder or eyepiece so that the photographer can see exactly what will be in the final picture. The most accurate viewfinders use mirrors to reflect the light, after it has come through the lens, to the viewfinder. When the photographer presses the button the mirror swings out of the way before the shutter opens.

Developing film

Once you have finished a roll of film, it must be developed. If you took the film out of its container in daylight and looked at it, you would see nothing interesting. The exposed film looks the same as it did before you put it in the camera. (And the daylight would spoil the film.) But when you took the picture the light altered the chemicals in the film so that they were ready for developing. During developing, special chemicals are used that turn the film dark in the places where light struck it. Places that were dark in the original image become transparent on the developed film. (This is for black and white film, colour is more complicated.) Even after a film has been developed it can still be spoiled by light, so the next step is to remove the chemicals in the film that can still be affected by light. This is called 'fixing' the film. Then the film is washed.

Negatives

You now have a negative. It is transparent and black and white but, as the name suggests, the dark and light areas are 'the wrong way round'. What was dark in the scene that you photographed is transparent in the negative, and what was bright in the scene is black in the negative.

Now the negative is placed over a piece of paper that has been coated with chemicals that are affected by light. This stage is carried out in darkness or in a very faint light that does not affect the paper. A light is switched on for a very short time. Then the paper is removed and developed and fixed just as the film was.

Where the negative was transparent, light passed through and affected the paper. Those parts of the paper become dark after they are developed – just as the same parts of the original scene were. The light could not pass through the dark parts of the negative, so those parts of the paper are light, as those parts of the original scene were. So after washing and drying the paper we have a picture of the scene we photographed, with dark and light areas in the right places.

Transparencies

Most photographs taken nowadays are colour pictures. One kind gives transparencies ('slides'). The film is coated with layers of chemicals that are transparent before the film is used, but become coloured after the film is developed. The result is that the film becomes red in areas where red light fell on it, yellow in places where yellow light hit it, and so on. That piece of film is cut from the roll and mounted in a square frame. The result is a transparent coloured picture of the original scene.

▼These are the processes involved in making a black and white photograph. Light rays from the subject are focused to form an image, which is preserved by a chemical change in the light-sensitive coating of the film. The film is then put, in the dark, into the developer in the light-tight tank. Next, the developer is poured away and other chemicals are poured on to 'stop' or neutralize the developer, and then to 'fix' the film. The negative is placed on to special paper, exposed very briefly to a bright light and then the paper is developed just as the film from the camera was.

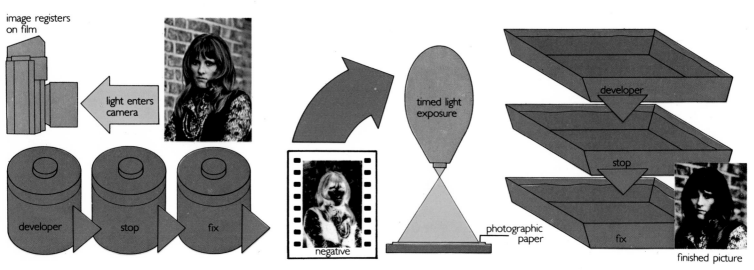

image registers on film

light enters camera

developer   stop   fix

negative

timed light exposure

developer

stop

photographic paper

fix

finished picture

Colour negatives

Another kind of film is called 'colour negative' film. After it has been developed the film shows the opposite colours to those of the original scene – yellow instead of blue, bluish green instead of red, and so on. To get a picture with the right colours, it is necessary to make a print, just as with the black and white film. But this time the paper has to be coated with chemicals that will become coloured after developing and printing.

'Instant' cameras

'Instant' cameras, such as those made by the Polaroid company, use a special film that contains its own developing and fixing chemicals. When the film is pulled from the camera, or pushed out by a built-in motor, these chemicals start working and produce the finished picture within seconds.

LENSES

Almost any device that uses light in some way has at least one lens in it. There is a lens on the front of your camera and in film and television cameras. There are lenses in car headlights, in binoculars and telescopes, and in many scientific instruments. Lenses are very useful because they can bend light rays.

At its simplest a lens is just a curved piece of glass or other transparent material, such as clear plastic. Very accurate lenses are made by grinding a thick flat disc of glass into the right shape. But lenses for car headlights, torches and the cheaper cameras are made by pouring hot liquid plastic into moulds and letting it set.

A lens may have one flat face and one curved one, or it may have two curved faces. A curved face may be convex, which means that it comes outwards in the middle, making the lens thicker in the middle than at the edges. Or it may be concave, meaning it goes inwards in the middle, making the lens thicker at the edges than in the middle. There are also lenses that have a concave face on one side and convex one on the other.

▲ Magnifying glasses are convex lenses. These two have different degrees of magnification because the lenses have different amounts of curve. The magnifying glass with low magnification has a lens that is only slightly curved, the more powerful one has a strongly curved lens.

The easiest type of lens to understand is one that is convex on both sides. A simple magnifying glass is an example. If you take a magnifying glass and a piece of paper out of doors on a sunny day, you can quickly see how the lens affects light rays. Hold the lens so that it faces the sun and sunlight goes through it onto the paper. By moving the lens nearer to the paper or farther away from it, you will find that at one position a bright spot of light is formed on the paper. This spot is a tiny image of the sun – a picture of it. The lens has focused the rays of sunlight – brought them to a point.

As you will quickly see, it has also focused the heat rays – the *infra-red* rays – in the sunlight. If you hold the glass and paper still, the paper will become so hot at the bright spot that it will start to smoulder.

If you bring the glass and the paper indoors, you can find out more about how images are formed. Hold the lens facing something bright, such as a window or an electric light. By moving the paper and lens you will find that you can get a

▼A real image, such as this one formed by a convex lens, can be 'caught' on a screen.

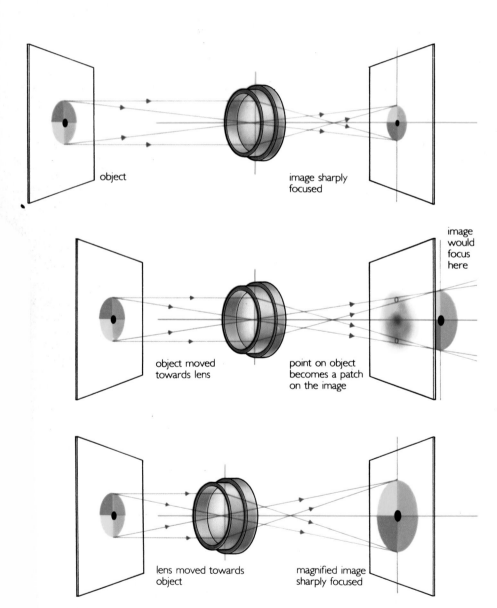

object

image sharply focused

image would focus here

object moved towards lens

point on object becomes a patch on the image

lens moved towards object

magnified image sharply focused

sharp image of the window or light. If you look carefully at it, you will notice that it is upside down.

You could use a lens like this in a camera to form an image on the film. Some cheap cameras do use simple single lenses. But they do not give very good images – they are slightly blurred. So good cameras use several lenses joined in a row one behind the other to make a 'compound' lens.

There are two main reasons why a simple lens gives a fuzzy image. One is that rays of light going through the edges of the lens are not focused to exactly the same point as rays going through the centre of the lens. In a simple camera this problem is avoided by blocking out the light near the edges of the lens.

The second reason is that a simple lens does not focus light of different colours at exactly the same place. The light from the sun, an electric light or a candle is a mixture of different colours.

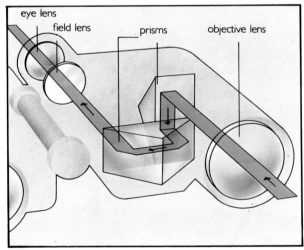

eye lens · field lens · prisms · objective lens

◄The size and quality of the image on a screen depends on the position of the lens in relation to the object and the screen. The image may be smaller than the object (top), or larger (bottom). If the object is moved towards the lens, the screen image becomes blurred.

▲Each side of a pair of binoculars contains a series of lenses that can magnify the objects being viewed by up to ten times. But the image is upside down and reversed. To make the image right for viewing, two prisms at right angles to each other bend the light and turn the image the right way up and the right way round.

Sunlight literally contains all the colours of the rainbow – for a rainbow is formed when raindrops split up sunlight into its colours. When light from the sun or an electric light passes through a simple lens, the blue part of the light forms an image close to the lens, and the red part forms an image farther away. Other colours in the light form images in between. If you look carefully at the image made by a magnifying glass, you will see that the edge of the window or light bulb has coloured fringes. Fortunately, scientists have found that they can make lenses that do not have this fault. They do it by making the lens from two or more smaller lenses, each made of different types of glass. The resulting lens focuses light of all colours at the same point.

There is a different way of using a magnifying glass. You can hold it close to, say, a piece of newspaper and look through it. The print on the newspaper will look larger – it will be 'magnified' – and it will be easier to read.

Lenses in glasses

Lenses are used in glasses. To understand how they help people to see more clearly, we must know how our eyes form pictures of the things around us. In the front of the eye there is a simple lens, which focuses light to form images on the back of the eye – the 'retina'. Muscles attached to the lens can make it change its shape. When they make the lens more rounded, it bends light more strongly; when it is flatter, it bends light less strongly. The lens needs to bend light strongly when it is trying to form a sharp image of nearby objects.

When somebody is 'far-sighted', they can see distant things clearly, but their eyes cannot form sharp images of nearby objects. The lenses in their eyes can focus only weakly. Spectacles using convex lenses, like magnifying glasses, can help them. They partly focus the light rays before they reach the wearer's eyes. The lenses inside the eyes can then finish the job of focusing the rays.

When somebody is 'near-sighted', they have the opposite problem. The lenses in their eyes focus too strongly. They can form images of nearby objects, but not of distant ones. The glasses that correct this fault have lenses with concave surfaces. This type of lens does not bring light rays to a point – it makes them spread out more. Then, when the spreading light rays pass through the lens in the eye, they are brought to a focus at the right place.

Because lenses with concave surfaces do not bring light rays to a focus, you cannot use one to form an image of the sun on a piece of paper. So you cannot do the experiments described earlier with the spectacles of a near-sighted person.

'Blooming' a lens

Cameras, telescopes and microscopes have several lenses inside them. This can cause problems because every time light enters or leaves a lens, some of it is reflected back. (Your reflection in a shop window is produced by light that is reflected from the glass of the window instead of going through it.) These reflections make the final image fainter and can spoil it. So lenses are coated with a very thin film of transparent material which reduces the reflections. This is called 'blooming' the lenses, and gives a purplish shine to them. You may be able to see the bloom on your camera lens, if it is a high-quality one.

▼Glasses have been worn since medieval times, although some of those early ones may have done the wearer's eyes more harm than good. Today's lenses are made to the individual's needs and frames come in a great range of styles and colours, very different from the wire contraptions of only a century ago.

MOTION PICTURES

▲Shooting a scene on location. Stunt scenes like this require a great deal of skill. When the sunlight is not bright enough for good photographs, strong lights are mounted on the camera truck.

▶Animated films like the *Pink Panther* are made up of thousands of drawings showing all the different movements made by each character. The finished drawings are photographed in the order they will be seen in the finished film.

Every time we go to the cinema to see a film, we are tricked by an optical illusion. We think we see things moving on the screen, but we are really looking at a series of still pictures.

The film is thrown onto the screen by a beam of light from a projector behind the audience. The film is a long strip of transparent pictures, usually in colour. The film was produced by a camera that normally takes 24 pictures a second, and the projector must show them at the same rate. A motor moves the film through the projector in jerks, stopping it to show one picture and then shutting off the light beam while the film moves on. There is a spinning shutter rather like a miniature fan to cut out the light. There is a 'claw' with teeth that fit into slots along the edge of the film and pull it along.

If the film were run slowly, you would see each picture appear on the screen, one after the other, with a moment of darkness in between. Each picture would be still, but from one picture to the next there would be slight changes in the positions of moving objects or people. When the film is shown at its proper speed we do not notice the moments of darkness, because they are so short, and the pictures seem to blend into a moving scene.

The camera that takes the film also has a claw system that jerks the film through at 24 frames per second. (A frame is another name for the pictures that make up the film.) When the film stops for a moment, a shutter opens and an image is focused onto the film by a lens at the front of the camera – just as in an ordinary camera.

Faster and slower

Sometimes the film camera takes pictures at a faster rate than 24 frames per second – perhaps a hundred times as fast, or even more. When the film is shown at the

36

►Part of a film strip of some sweets being made. Although the sweets look convincingly real, the film was actually made using models.

normal rate, there will be a slow motion effect. You can see an explosion, for example, occurring very slowly.

But sometimes film-makers want to speed up the action – to make a car chase more exciting, for example. To do this the camera takes pictures at a slower rate than 24 frames per second. When it is projected at the normal rate, everything seems speeded up.

Film sound tracks

The sound on a major cinema film is nearly always recorded after the filming. This is because it is very difficult to make good recordings of good quality outside the studio. For one thing, it is difficult to get microphones near the actors yet out of the camera's view.

When the sound is eventually recorded, it is put onto a 'sound track', which runs along the edge of the film, alongside the pictures. The sound track looks like a pattern of clear and dark bands in the film. A light is shone through it as the film runs. The light that comes through the film varies in strength according to the lightness or darkness of the sound track. The light beam is turned into an electric current of varying strength, which is finally turned into sounds that match the sounds originally recorded. The sound recording must be very carefully made so that the sound fits the action. The actors' voices, for example, must fit the movements of their lips on the screen.

▲This is how the film of the sweets was made. One model is shown ready for photographing with the camera on the right. A whole series of models was photographed (you can see some of them in the background of the picture). Each one had the ribbons of 'toffee' and the 'chocolate' in slightly different positions. When the film is run the 'toffee' seems to pour into the 'chocolate' mould, just as the machines actually do it in a sweet factory. Making movements on film using still objects like these is called animation.

MIRRORS

You may have noticed how many different kinds of mirror there are. There are the ordinary flat ones that you look at yourself in while washing or while trying on clothes in a shop. There are magnifying mirrors that people use while shaving or putting on make-up. There are the rear-view mirrors in cars, which often give a wide-angle view of the road behind. There are curved mirrors in car headlights and pocket torches, which focus the light into a beam. And there are the distorting mirrors in fairgrounds, which make you look as if your body is strangely stretched in one part and squashed in another. How do all these different kinds of mirror work?

A mirror is very smooth and shiny. And almost any very shiny surface can act as a mirror. You can see a reflection of yourself in a polished spoon, in a window, and in the surface of a bowl of water. In ancient Egypt, more than 5000 years ago, pieces of flat polished metal were used as mirrors. A modern mirror consists of a very thin layer of silver coated onto the back of a piece of glass, which protects the silver.

The reflections of people and objects that you can see in a mirror are called 'images', which means 'pictures'. To understand how mirrors form images, we must think about what happens to light

▼This huge glass mirror, protected within a metal ring, is being moved before work on it is finished. It measures 370 cm (12 ft) in diameter and weighs 13 tons. Its surface will be coated with a thin film of aluminium so it will reflect as much light as possible. Then it will be mounted as the main mirror in the European Southern Observatory on top of La Silla Mountain in Chile.

▶Try placing a concave mirror on a table and shining a light into it. Different patters will form on the table according to where the light is.

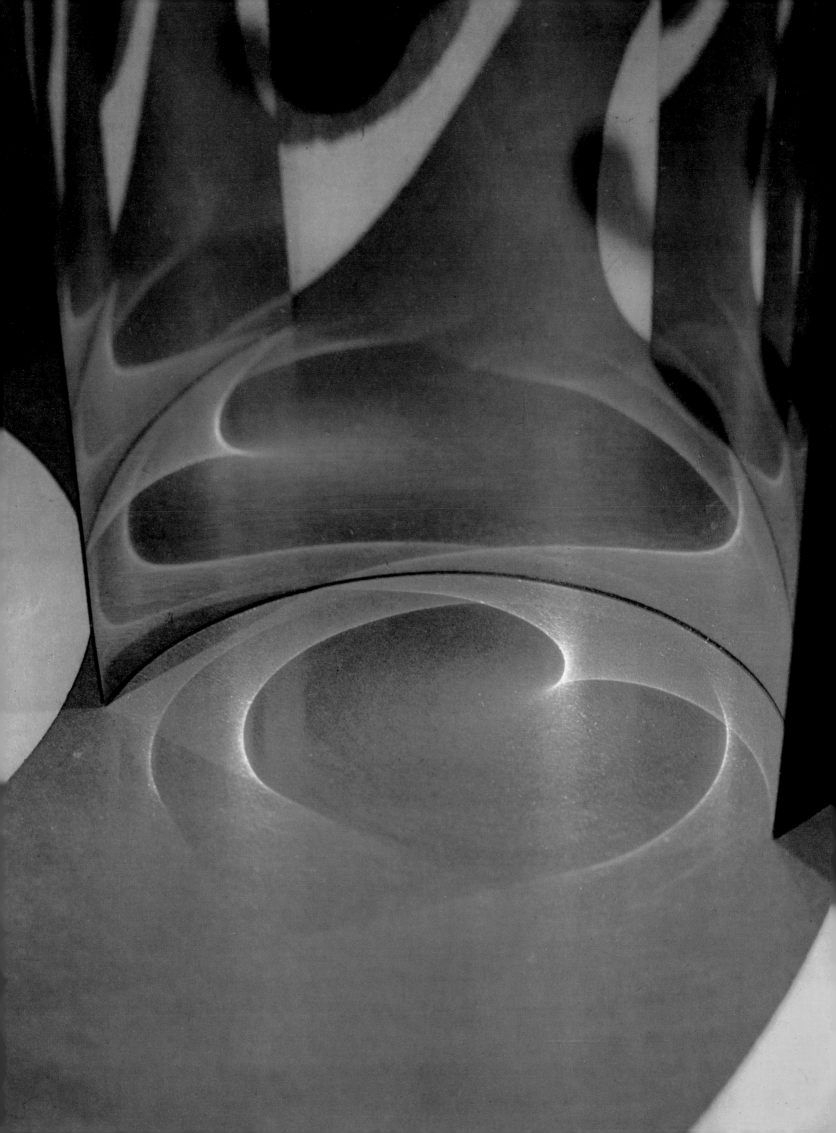

rays when they strike a mirror. We see an object when light rays reflected from the surface of the object reach our eyes. The direction that the light rays have come from tells us the direction of the object. If some of the light rays from the object hit a mirror, they bounce off it and start travelling in a different direction – like a ball bouncing off a wall. If the light rays from the mirror reach your eye, it's as if you were seeing light from the object itself. But this new 'object' seems to be behind the mirror, because that's the place that the reflected rays are spreading from. This new 'object' is an image formed by the mirror. We say that it's an image *of* the original object – a picture of it.

Light rays from the object could also hit a wall and be reflected from that. But the surface of the wall is so rough that the reflected rays would not travel in one definite direction. They would be jumbled and would not look as if they were coming from an image of the object.

The images you see in a flat mirror are as far behind the mirror as the objects are in front of it. And they are the same size as the objects. Curved mirrors produce different sorts of images.

Concave mirrors

There are two kinds of curved mirror. A shiny spoon will show you both types. The inside of the bowl is a *concave* mirror – it curves away from you in the middle (like a cave). If you look at yourself in the bowl of the spoon, you will see an upside-down image of your face, and it will seem to be just in *front* of the spoon. This is because the concave surface of the bowl has reflected the light rays from your face inwards towards one place – it has focused the rays. After coming together, the light rays travel on and reach your eye. Because the rays are spreading from the place at which they were focused, you see an image of your face at that point. The image is upside down because the rays crossed over each other as they travelled from the spoon to your eye.

A shaving mirror or makeup mirror is also concave. If you look at one of these from a distance, you will see just what you saw when you looked in the spoon. But if you get closer to the mirror, you will not see an upside-down image, because the light rays will reach your eyes before they can come to a focus. You will now see an image the right way up and behind the mirror. But because the rays are converging (coming closer together) they look as if they are coming from a magnified image of your face.

Convex mirrors

The other kind of curved mirror is *convex*. It curves towards you in the middle. The back of a polished spoon makes a convex mirror. You can see an image of yourself in it, but it is reduced in size. You can also see more of the room reflected in it than when you look in the concave side of the spoon. That is why convex mirrors are often used for drivers' rear-view mirrors – they give a good view of the road behind the car. But distances seem to be reduced in the mirror, so a driver can make mistakes before he or she gets used to it.

When light rays spread out from an object and bounce off a convex mirror, the curvature of the mirror makes them spread more widely. The reflected rays seem to be coming from a place that is just behind the surface of the mirror.

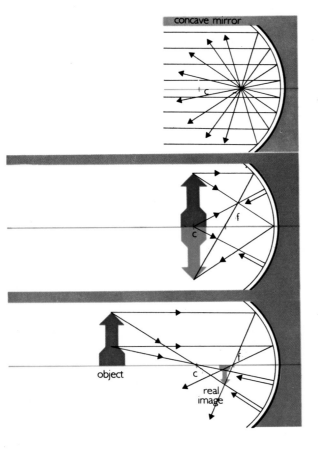

◀In a concave mirror the light rays are reflected to meet at **f**, the focus. The centre of the curving surface, **c**, is the centre of the sphere of which the mirror is a part. When the object to be reflected is at **c**, the image, also at **c**, is real and inverted (upside down). When the object is beyond **c**, a real, but smaller, inverted image is formed.

That is why the images seem to be only a little way behind the mirror. And all the distances are reduced, which is why the images are small.

The distorting mirrors in amusement parks are convex in some parts and concave in others. That is how they squeeze and stretch your image.

A concave mirror can be used to form an image on a piece of paper. Hold a concave shaving mirror or makeup mirror so that it faces a window or electric light. Move the paper backwards and forwards in front of the mirror. When the paper is at the right position, an upside-down image of the window or light will be formed on it. The largest astronomical telescopes use concave mirrors in this way. A giant mirror, as much as 6 m (20 ft) across, forms an image of, say, a planet. It is upside down, but that is not important when you are looking at a planet. The image can be photographed or studied through an eyepiece which is essentially a microscope. This kind of telescope is called a 'reflecting telescope' or 'reflector'.

If a beam of parallel light rays is shone straight at a concave mirror, they will be brought together at one point. If, instead, a light is placed at that point, the light rays from it will be reflected to form a parallel beam. This is what the concave mirrors in car headlights and torches do.

When a concave mirror has to be very accurate – in a telescope or a searchlight, for example – it has to be a special shape.

Seen from the side, the shape is not part of a circle, but of a curve called a parabola. In a telescope, a parabolic mirror forms very sharp images. And in a searchlight the mirror focuses the light rays into an absolutely parallel beam.

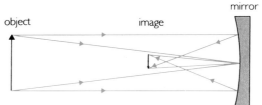
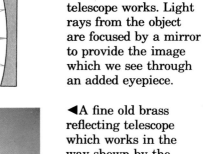

◄Diagram showing how a reflector telescope works. Light rays from the object are focused by a mirror to provide the image which we see through an added eyepiece.

◄A fine old brass reflecting telescope which works in the way shown by the diagram above. The tiny 'telescope' on the top of the main one is a 'finder'. The observer uses it to find the object that is to be observed before setting the main telescope.

▼The reflector at the observatory of Merate in Italy has a mirror 100cm (40in) in diameter.

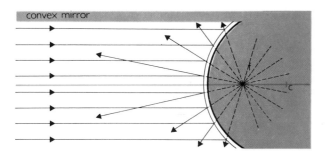

▲In a convex mirror the light rays are reflected so that they spread out. The rays seem to come from being focused behind the mirror.

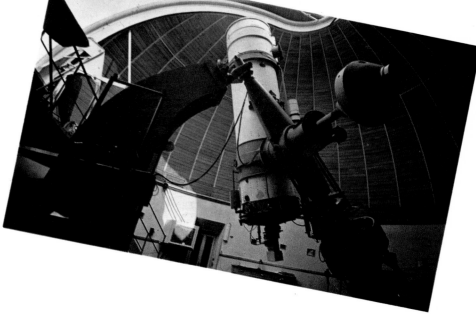
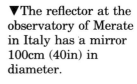

4 SOUNDWAVES WORKING

RADIO

The old name for radio was 'wireless'. It was called this because the signal – the words and music – travels from the broadcasting station to the receiving set without any connecting wires between the two. The signal travels by radio waves.

Radio waves

Radio waves are waves of electricity and magnetism, and they can travel through empty space. This is why we can send radio messages to distant space probes and receive signals back from them.

To understand radio waves, we have to understand the word 'frequency'. Think of waves on the sea, moving past a stationary boat. The frequency of the waves is the number of waves that pass every second. The frequency of a radio wave is the number of radio waves that pass every second. You cannot see radio waves – you have to detect them with a radio receiver.

The frequency of the waves used in radio broadcasting are much higher than the frequency of an ocean wave. A million or a hundred million waves per second are typical frequencies.

At the broadcasting station there is a large antenna (also called an aerial). The radio waves travel out from this antenna in all directions. They can be 'picked up', or detected, by the antenna of the radio receiver. This can be a metal rod inside the radio receiver. But for VHF (very high frequency) waves, a long antenna is needed. This can be mounted on the outside of your house. Or it can be an

▼A radio receiver made in 1943 – how clumsy it looks beside today's Walkman! But the 1943 set was quite the latest, most up-to-date equipment in its time. What will replace the Walkman, making that, in its turn, look clumsy and old-fashioned?

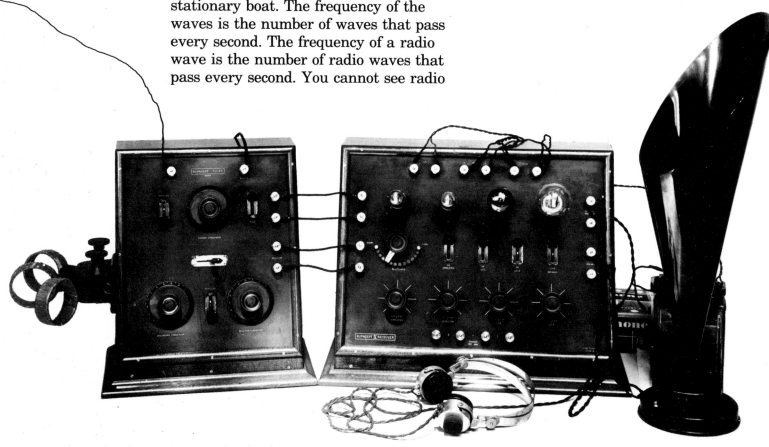

extending rod fitted to the outside of a portable radio. Car radios always need an antenna fitted to the outside of the car, because radio waves cannot travel through the metal car body.

As the radio waves hit the antenna, they make tiny electrical currents flow in the metal. These currents are led by a wire to the rest of the radio set, which converts them to sound.

The radio wave is really a combination of two kinds of wave. One is a steady 'carrier' wave. The frequency of this wave is called the frequency of the transmitter. It is the frequency that the radio receiver must be tuned to. If you turn the dial on your radio and tune it to a different frequency, you will hear a different station.

The other part of the radio wave carries the signal representing the sounds. In the broadcasting studio sounds are turned into electric currents by microphones. The currents vary rapidly, in the same pattern as the loudness of the sounds. These electric currents are then used to add the sound-carrying wave to the carrier radio wave.

Amplitude modulation

There are two ways of doing this. The first method is to use the sound signal to change the strength of the carrier wave. Imagine you are watching ocean waves go past. The height of the waves is their strength. If you saw the waves getting stronger and stronger as each one went

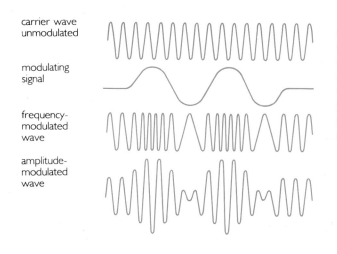

carrier wave unmodulated

modulating signal

frequency-modulated wave

amplitude-modulated wave

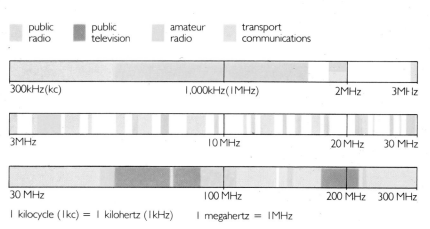

public radio	public television	amateur radio	transport communications

300kHz(kc) 1,000kHz(1MHz) 2MHz 3MHz

3MHz 10MHz 20MHz 30MHz

30 MHz 100 MHz 200 MHz 300 MHz

1 kilocycle (1kc) = 1 kilohertz (1kHz)   1 megahertz = 1MHz

◄Each radio station transmits a carrier wave. Sounds to be transmitted are changed into signals which alter (modulate) the frequency or amplitude of the carrier current.

past, then dying away and then building up again, they would give you an idea of what this type of radio wave is like. The changes in the strength of the carrier wave represent the varying loudness of the words and music. This method of adding the sound signal to the carrier wave is called amplitude modulation – AM for short. 'Amplitude' means 'strength' and 'modulation' means

▲Many people use radio for communication. Each group of users has a particular range of wavebands to use for broadcasting. This ensures that, for example, public radio broadcasts do not get mixed up with those of amateur radio enthusiasts.

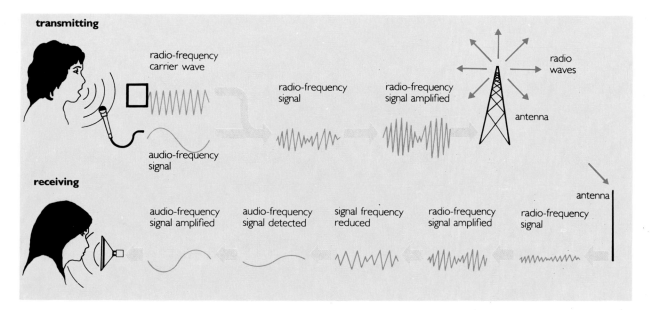

transmitting

radio-frequency carrier wave

audio-frequency signal

radio-frequency signal

radio-frequency signal amplified

radio waves

antenna

receiving

audio-frequency signal amplified

audio-frequency signal detected

signal frequency reduced

radio-frequency signal amplified

radio-frequency signal

antenna

◄Diagram showing how a radio transmitter and reciver work. The carrier wave, modulated by the sound (audio) signal, is sent into the air by the transmitting antenna as amplified waves. The waves weaken as they spread out through the air. The receiving antenna picks up the weakened waves. These are then amplified by the radio equipment. The sound signal is picked out and changed back into sounds.

43

▲Radio serves aircraft both as a means of communication and navigation. Radio waves are sent out in pulses and are reflected by the land or sea below. By comparing the echoes with signals received by a special radio set, a navigator can find both his speed and direction. Another radio navigation system uses a kind of 'radio map'. Navigation systems using radio are extremely useful because they can be used in any weather and are the basis of the 'blind landing' systems used to land aircraft when visibility is bad.

▶A radio disc jockey on the air. He wears earphones so that the programme's producer can speak to him without the conversation interrupting the broadcast.

'changing'. Part of your radio dial is marked AM, because that is where you have to tune your radio to receive AM broadcasts.

Frequency modulation

The other method is called frequency modulation, or FM. The varying loudness of the sounds is represented by changing the frequency of the carrier wave very slightly. FM gives very high-quality broadcasts, but it can be used only with VHF waves. VHF waves have only a

short range, so they are used by local radio stations. You will find these on a part of your radio dial marked FM or VHF/FM.

Amplifying the current

Inside the receiving set, the electrical currents from the antenna also consist of waves, with the same pattern as the radio waves. The currents consist of a part that has the same frequency as the carrier wave, and a part that varies in just the same way as the radio waves carrying words and music. The electronic circuits in the radio set ignore the carrier wave part of the electric current. The rest of the current, which is tiny, must be made much bigger. This is called 'amplifying' the current. After being amplified, the current is strong enough to make a loudspeaker in the set reproduce the original sounds. The current makes a paper or plastic cone vibrate, and the vibrations set up waves in the air. These sound waves have the same pattern as the original sounds at the radio station, and so it is just as if we are hearing the original words or music.

RECORD PLAYER

Sounds are waves, or vibrations, in the air. The pitch of the sound depends on the *frequency* of the waves that is, the number of vibrations per second. If 400 waves hit your eardrum every second, you will hear the note 'A'. If 256 waves reach you every second, you will hear 'middle C'. But the sounds we hear almost never consist of pure single frequencies. If a piano and a guitar both play middle C, the main frequency in the two sounds will be 256 waves per second, but there will be other frequencies as well, called 'overtones'. The differences between the overtones make the difference in the sounds of the two instruments. Using a low-quality record player, which does not reproduce all the overtones accurately, you may not be able to tell the difference between the guitar and the piano. But with good equipment you can. In fact, on the best modern tape and record players, it can be hard to tell whether you are listening to a recording or to the original sounds.

Good-quality recording is called 'hi-fi', which stands for 'high fidelity'. Fidelity is faithfulness, or accuracy. This accuracy must be present in the original recording – if that is not good, there is no point in having a good tape or record player.

Making a record
Many microphones are used when a recording is made in a studio. Each microphone produces an electric current that varies in just the same way as the sounds. So if a middle C is played, the current will surge back and forth 256 times a second. And there will be smaller fluctuations in the current, too, for all the overtones in the sound.

The electric current from each microphone is used to make a tape recording. This consists of a pattern of magnetic fields along the tape. The magnetism is like the magnetism of a compass needle. The strength of the magnetism varies along the tape, in a pattern that is again an exact copy of the original sound.

The recording engineers take the tape recordings from all the microphones and

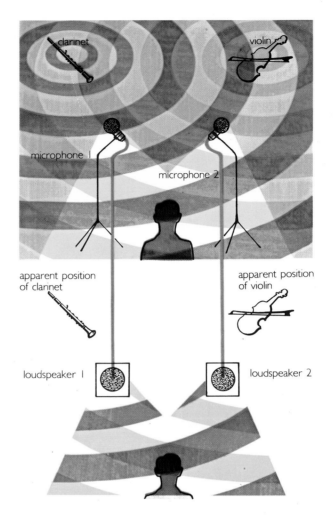

▶The principles of stereo recording can be shown like this, with the sound from the clarinet as the blue waves, and the sounds from the violin as yellow waves. The listener in the concert hall or the studio hears the clarinet louder in his left ear and the violin louder in his right ear (top), Microphones are specially placed to pick up both sounds. When the stereophonic reproduction is relayed to the listener elsewhere, through more specially placed loudspeakers, he hears the same sound as the listener in the concert hall.

use them to make a 'master' disc. The tape recordings control a needle as it cuts a groove in the disc. Usually parts of the recording where mistakes were made are left out, and only the best parts are used. The records that are sold in the shops are copies of the master disc. Cassette tapes with copies of the recording are also sold.

Nearly all recordings are stereophonic. This means that when you are listening to them it sounds as if the voices and instruments are spread out in front of you in different positions, just as they would have been if you had been in the recording studio. To get a stereophonic effect, you need to play the recordings through two loudspeakers. The speakers play slightly different sounds, so your ears hear slightly different things – just as they do when you are really present at, say, a concert. To achieve the effect a stereophonic disc has separate recordings for the two speakers – one in each side of the groove.

Playing a record

►Modern records, record players and recording methods are so good that the sound you hear is often more perfect than if you were actually at a concert. The earliest records often crackled so much when they were played it was difficult to hear the music.

▼The earliest records were mono. When a disc of this kind is cut, the cutter records an electrical signal by moving from side to side. The groove curves, but is the same depth and width along its length. When the disc is played, the pick-up head converts the movements of the stylus back into an electrical signal which can be changed into sound. Stereo discs are cut in a similar way, but the cutter records two signals from two sound sources by moving up and down as well as from side to side.

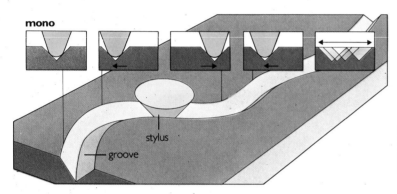

mono

stylus

groove

stereo

The playing equipment must be very accurate to get the benefits of hi-fi recording. The record turntable must rotate at exactly the right speed – 33⅓ or 45 times per minute, according to the type of record. If the speed of the record varies even slightly, musical notes will 'wobble'. This fault is called 'wow'.

The record player's pickup arm has a stylus, or needle, which follows the grooves in the disc. The vibration of the stylus are converted into electric currents.

The electric currents from a record player are too weak to make loudspeakers work. So they are sent to an amplifier, which makes them stronger. Again, the amplifier must be of good quality so that it does not change the pattern of the electric currents at all. If it does it will distort the sound.

The loudspeakers convert the amplified currents into sound waves. In most types there is a plastic cone, which is made to vibrate, sending out a complicated pattern of sound waves. The best hi-fi sets have four loudspeakers – one pair on the left and another on the right. Each pair consists of a large speaker, called a 'woofer', for the low notes, and a small one, called a 'tweeter', for the high ones.

Digital recording

Increasingly, recordings are being made by digital methods. 'Digital' means 'using numbers'. When the recording is made in the studio, the microphones give fluctuating electric currents, just as they do in ordinary sound recording. The difference is in the way the electric currents are stored on magnetic tape. The current is 'sampled' thousands of times every second, and its strength is measured as a number, which is stored on the tape. There are thousands of these numbers for every second of playing time. Each number is represented as a series of magnetic pulses by spaces. There is a different pattern of pulses and spaces for each number. It is rather like Morse code, which represents numbers (and letters of the alphabet) by patterns of long and short bleeps. This way of showing numbers is called *binary* notation. 'Binary' means 'based on two', and in binary notation all the information about the numbers is given by two types of signal – pulses and spaces.

Computers work with numbers in binary form, and the numbers stored on tape in a digital recording can be easily altered by special computers. This means that the adjustments that have to be made before the final master disc is produced can be very easily carried out. In the final record or tape, the sound is represented by a groove or by magnetism in just the same way as in an ordinary recording. The loudness of the sound varies from moment to moment according to the numbers stored on tape during the original recording, and so the original sound is reproduced. The quality of sound in a digital recording can be very high.

▲This digital sound recorder can record on 24 tracks at a time, although the recording tape is only 1.3cm (½in) wide. There are, in fact, another four tracks on the tape, but these are used for recording editing information and checking timing. This complicated machine depends on computerization, without it the high-quality recordings we are used to would be quite impossible to make.

Compact discs

The 'compact disc' is a new type of high-quality record. The sound is stored on a compact disc in digital form. Instead of a groove, there is a series of tiny pits, separated by spaces of varying sizes. A group of pulses and spaces represents the strength of the sound at a particular moment. Instead of a stylus, the record player uses a beam of laser light. This light is reflected from the surface of the disc in a different way according to whether or not one of the pits is passing underneath the pick-up. A light detector registers the reflected light and converts it into an electric current. The strength of the current from moment to moment depends on the information represented by the pattern of pits and spaces on the record. So the electric current coming from the record player is an accurate representation of the sound. The current is passed to an amplifier and then to loudspeakers in the usual way.

The compact disc is smaller than the usual long-playing record, and spins much faster – at about 250 rpm (revolutions per minute). Yet each side can play for an hour. The disc is made of

metal, coated in a protective layer of clear plastic. Minor scratches and dirt on the plastic do not affect the laser beam, so the record can be kept in perfect condition virtually for ever.

▲The records and record players we are used to are being challenged by even more modern techniques. The sound from this compact disc is 'picked up' by a laser, not a stylus.

47

TAPE RECORDER

The most common type of tape recorder is the 'cassette' recorder, in which the tape is enclosed in a plastic holder, the cassette. The tape is wound back and forth between two spools in the cassette. Larger tape recorders, for very high-quality recordings, use wider tape, which is wound on two separate reels mounted on the outside of the recorder. But all types of tape recorder work in the same way.

The tape is made of plastic, coated with particles of a material that can be magnetized. This material may be a compound of iron or of chromium.

The recorder has a motor, run by batteries or mains electricity, which unwinds the tape from one spool and winds it onto the other. Let us first see what happens when a recording is made.

Recording
The tape moves steadily past a 'recording head'. This is an electromagnet – a device that becomes a magnet when an electric current flows through it but is unmagnetized when no current flows. During recording, a rapidly varying current comes from the microphone to the recording head. The current is controlled by the sound waves – vibrations in the air – reaching the microphone, and its strength varies in just the same way as

the loudness of the sounds. It is a kind of copy in electricity of the sound waves.

The magnetism of the recording head magnetizes the tape as it goes by. (Just as you can magnetize an iron nail by stroking it with a magnet.) So there is a pattern of changing magnetism along the tape after it has passed the recording head.

Playback
Playback is the opposite of recording. The tape is moved past a 'playback head'. As it goes past it sets up a varying electric current in a small coil of wire in the playback head. This current is an exact copy of the current produced by the microphone during recording. The current is made bigger by an *amplifier* and can be used to drive a loudspeaker. This produces vibrations in the air that are a copy of the sounds that reached the microphone during the recording (see Record Player page 45).

Stereophonic tape recorders
Tape recorders that are stereophonic use two microphones and have two recordings, slightly different from each other, running side by side along the tape. Each recording is played through a separate loudspeaker or headphone, and so the listener's left and right ears hear slightly different sounds. This gives the sound a spread-out '3-D' quality.

When a tape recording is made, all traces of magnetism that may previously have been on the tape must be removed. This is done by an 'erase' head, which the tape passes immediately before it reaches the recording head. The erase head produces a strong magnetic field that constantly reverses in direction and wipes out any previous recording.

5 ELECTRONICS – A WHOLE NEW WORLD

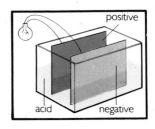

►How a very simple wet cell is made. Two metal plates are dipped into a container of acid. When the plates are joined a current flows.

BATTERY

►Two very early cells used in some of the first experiments with batteries. Each of these cells gave only one or, at the most, two volts. Once scientists realized that by linking cells they could create a stronger voltage and therefore a brighter light, the way was open for making much more powerful and useful batteries.

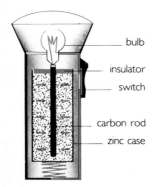

▲The electricity to light a flashlight or torch is provided by a 'dry' cell. The cell is not absolutely dry, because it contains a damp paste, as well as the central carbon rod, within the zinc case. When the switch is moved to 'on', a current of electricity flows in a circuit between the rod and the case, and the wire in the bulb glows white-hot, so giving off the light we see.

A battery is a device that generates electrical current from chemical reactions. In the simplest type of battery, such as a torch or flashlight battery, the current is generated by dissolving a metal in an acid or other chemical. The battery consists of a carbon zinc 'cup' containing a paste made of several chemicals. In the centre is a carbon rod. The whole battery is contained in a case of another metal covered with cardboard or paint, and there is a brass or steel cap on top of the carbon rod. the carbon rod and the zinc case are called the 'poles' of the battery. Every battery has two poles. The carbon and the zinc each have a piece of brass connected to them, called a terminal. The two terminals are visible at the top of the battery. When the terminals are connected by a wire, the battery begins to operate. The zinc begins to dissolve in the paste; and an electric current flows through the battery and along the wire.

In a torch the wire connecting the terminals is arranged so that the current flows through a light bulb as it travels from one terminal to the other. The current consists of huge numbers of tiny particles, called *electrons*. As they move along they bump against the *atoms* of which the wire is made and create heat. In the light bulb the wire is made of the metal tungsten. The current heats up the tungsten and makes it glow brightly.

When you switch the torch off, a gap is made in the wire connecting the battery's terminals. The electric current cannot flow across the gap. So the current stops, and so does the chemical reaction.

After a few hours' use, the zinc and other chemicals are used up and stop producing electricity. The battery should be taken out of the torch then, in case acid leaks out and spoils it.

The proper name for a simple battery is 'cell'. The word 'battery' should really only be used for a number of cells linked together. The flat battery used in some bicycle lamps is made of three cells linked together. This is done to give a larger current. The 'strength' with which a cell or battery can make a current flow is called its voltage, and is measured in volts. Each torch cell gives only a small voltage – about 1½ volts. When three of them are linked together, the voltage is three times as big and this helps to make the light brighter.

Most torch batteries must be thrown away after they have been used for a short while. But some batteries can be used again if electricity is passed through them in the reverse direction. The electricity can come from the main sockets in the home. This process is called 'recharging'. Car batteries are designed to be recharged by the car engine. The engine drives a device called a 'dynamo' or 'alternator', which produces electricity at a higher voltage than the battery does. The dynamo forces electricity through the battery and this reverses the chemical reaction. The battery is then ready to produce electricity again. The battery is used to start the engine and to run the lights and other electrical devices in the car.

A car battery is made in quite a different way from a torch battery, in order to make it rechargeable. The poles consist of two sets of rectangular metal plates. One set of plates is coated with lead. The other is coated with lead dioxide. The acid is a liquid – sulphuric acid.

Different kinds of battery

Different kinds of battery are needed for different tasks. A car battery is heavy and filled with liquid. It works very well in a car, but would be useless for a torch which needs a battery that is light in weight and has no liquid that can be spilled. Hearing aids, calculators and artificial limbs that are electrically powered need small, powerful batteries. These devices use 'mercury' batteries. One pole of this kind of battery consists of mercuric oxide and carbon, and the other is made of zinc. Mercury batteries are small and supply a steady current until they run out. Ordinary batteries usually get gradually weaker over a long period. But mercury batteries are more expensive than ordinary ones.

All the batteries that have been described so far use up their chemicals and eventually stop working. But space scientists have invented a battery that is continually supplied with chemicals. This is called a 'fuel cell'. The kind that is used in a space craft uses the gases hydrogen and oxygen instead of the zinc and acid of a torch battery. Fuel cells will continue to run as long as hydrogen and oxygen are supplied. They have the extra advantage for spacecraft that they produce water, which the astronauts need in space.

An end to vehicle fumes?

Nowadays scientists are trying to invent batteries that are as good as the car battery but much lighter. They would like to use these new batteries in electric cars, which are silent and do not produce poisonous exhaust gases. But at present

electric cars are slow and cannot go far before the battery needs to be recharged. This is because car batteries are now so heavy that the car uses up a lot of energy just carrying them. New lightweight batteries could make clean, quiet electric cars part of our everyday lives.

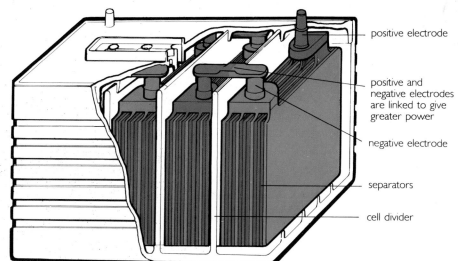

▲ positive electrode

positive and negative electrodes are linked to give greater power

negative electrode

separators

cell divider

▲ This diagram shows how a vehicle battery is made. Each cell has positive and negative plates placed in layers, rather like sandwiches. The cells are then linked up to give the strength of current needed for a vehicle.

▲ Batteries are so much a part of modern life that we take them for granted – only noticing them when they are flat. Think about the number of things in your home that need batteries. You'll probably be surprised how many there are.

WATCHES AND CLOCKS

►The mechanism of a spring watch is the same in principle as that of a clock, but all the parts are, of course, much smaller. The winder tightens the mainspring. As it uncoils the mainspring turns the main wheel. This drives the centre wheel which carries the minute hand. The speed of the centre wheel is controlled by the escape wheel, through the third and fourth wheels. The escape wheel is controlled in turn by the vibration of the hairspring, through the balance wheel and lever. The hardest steels are used for the wheels and jewels for some of the bearings.

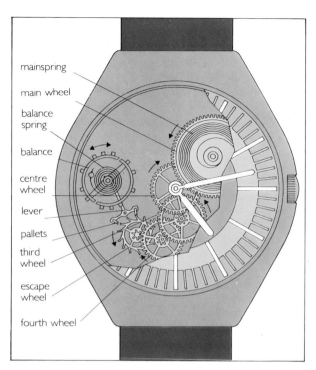

- mainspring
- main wheel
- balance spring
- balance
- centre wheel
- lever
- pallets
- third wheel
- escape wheel
- fourth wheel

At the heart of an electric watch is a tiny crystal of quartz, together with a *microchip* and other electronic components. Quartz, like other crystals, vibrates with a regular beat, rather like a bell but very much faster – between 6,000 and 40,000 times a second. An electric battery in the watch keeps the quartz crystal vibrating.

Quartz is unusual: it is a *piezoelectric* material. This means that, whenever it is forced to change shape, it produces a small electric current. So as the crystal vibrates, each quiver produces a tiny electric current that is passed to the microchip. The chip is a tiny computer that counts the pulses of current and converts them into much slower ones – perhaps one every hundredth of a second.

On a digital watch the chip also makes the current produce numbers on the face. If the watch is being used as a stopwatch, the hundredths of a second will be displayed. The watch also shows tenths of a second. The chip counts the hundredths of a second and after every ten of them displays another tenth of a second. After every ten tenths of a second it shows another second as having passed. When you use the watch in the normal way, not as a stopwatch, the hundredths and tenths are not displayed. Instead you see seconds, minutes and hours. Usually the

watch can also show the day of the week and the date – even making allowance for leap years.

Some people prefer 'analogue' watches. This is the scientific name for watches with hands. In an analogue watch the electrical pulses produced by the microchip are used to drive an electric motor so that the hand that marks seconds moves round in jumps, one each second. The motor also drives the minute and hour hands by means of a system of gears, so that they move at the correct rate.

Clockwork watches

Before the quartz-controlled electronic watch became available, most watches were driven by clockwork. The clockwork was moved by a spring, which had to be wound up by the watch's owner each day. But on some watches the spring was wound automatically by the normal everyday movements of the person wearing the watch.

If the watch were as simple as that, it

▲Testing a cesium 'atomic' clock in a laboratory. These clocks measure time by comparing the frequency of vibrating cesium atoms. Because the frequency is constant, clocks like these are accurate within one second in 30,000 years!

would run more and more slowly as the spring unwound. So the movement of the hands was regulated by a 'balance wheel'. This was a wheel, connected to a spring, which spun backwards and forwards. Each swing of the wheel took exactly the same time. With each swing of the balance wheel the system of gears in the watch moved by one notch. So the balance wheel ensured that the watch kept good time.

Clocks

Small clocks used balance wheels, just like watches. But bigger clocks were controlled by pendulums – gently swinging weights. When a pendulum swings, each swing takes exactly the same time. Some pendulum clocks were driven by springs. Others were driven by a weight on a string. The weight would slowly descend and would have to be pulled up again from time to time.

The most important other kind of clock, which is still used a great deal, is the electric clock. This is driven by electricity from the main house current, which is not a steady current but a series of pulses.

There are 60 pulses a second in some countries, 50 a second in others. An electric clock converts these into a slower series of pulses which turn the hands.

◄The face of a combined LCD (liquid crystal display) analogue and digital quartz watch. It runs for about three years on a single silver-oxide power cell, and it flashes when a replacement cell is needed.

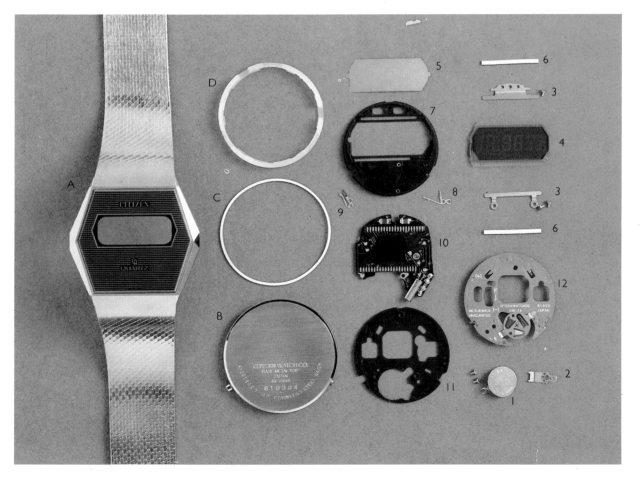

◄The parts needed to make a slim-line LCD quartz watch.
A watch case with band
B case back
C packing for case back
D movement holder
1 unit of power cell
2 power cell connector
3 LCD panel holder
4 LCD panel
5 reflecting plate
6 LCD panel connection rubber
7 LCD panel support
8 display change-over switch spring
9 switch spring for correction
10 plate complete
11 supporter for plate complete (1)
12 supporter for plate complete (2)

TRANSISTOR

▲Three different sizes of portable radio, but they all rely on transistors. Like computers, modern radios are much smaller than the originals, while doing their work better.

Your radio receives only a tiny electric current from its antenna (aerial). This current has to be increased, or 'amplified', to make it strong enough to power a loudspeaker. The amplifying is done by transistors – tiny electronic components inside the radio. Transistors are just as important in television sets. And a computer contains thousands upon thousands of transistors.

An electric current consists of a stream of *electrons*. These are tiny particles, much smaller than an atom. Each one carries a negative electric charge. One terminal of a battery, called the negative pole, supplies a stream of electrons. This terminal is marked with a '−' or minus sign. The other terminal is called the positive pole, and is marked with a '+' or plus sign. This is where electrons flow back into the battery after travelling through an electrical device, such as a light bulb or a radio. In a metal wire there are millions of electrons that can move easily, so a wire is a good 'conductor' of electricity. But transistors

are made from materials such as germanium or silicon, which do not have many free electrons. Such materials are called 'semiconductors' because they do not conduct electricity easily.

Semiconductors
Crystals of semiconducting material are grown artificially in factories. To make the semiconductor useful for transistors, it must be 'doped' with another material in tiny, carefully controlled quantities. For example, a tiny amount of arsenic may be added to a crystal of germanium. Electrons from the arsenic become separated from their atoms and wander around the germanium. All atoms in their normal state are made up of some particles that are negatively charged and others that are positively charged, so the two kinds of charge cancel each other out. When an electron is separated from the arsenic atom, there is an unbalanced positive charge in the atom. But this positive charge is fixed in position because the atom cannot move.

Germanium doped with arsenic is called an 'n-type' semiconductor because only the 'negative-type' charges – the electrons – can move.

It is also possible to have 'p-type' semiconductors. An example is germanium doped with atoms of gallium. Each gallium atom 'steals' an electron from a nearby germanium atom. That germanium atom now has an unbalanced positive charge. Soon an electron from another germanium atom jumps into the first atom, cancelling out its positive charge, but leaving an unbalanced positive charge on the atom it has left. It is just as if a positive charge has jumped from the first to the second atom. So we talk of positive charges moving through the crystal and call it a p-type semiconductor. But really these are negatively charged electrons moving in the opposite direction to the imaginary 'movement' of the positive charges.

Diodes
To understand how a transistor works, we first need to know how a simpler device, called a diode, works. A piece of n-type semiconductor is joined to a piece of

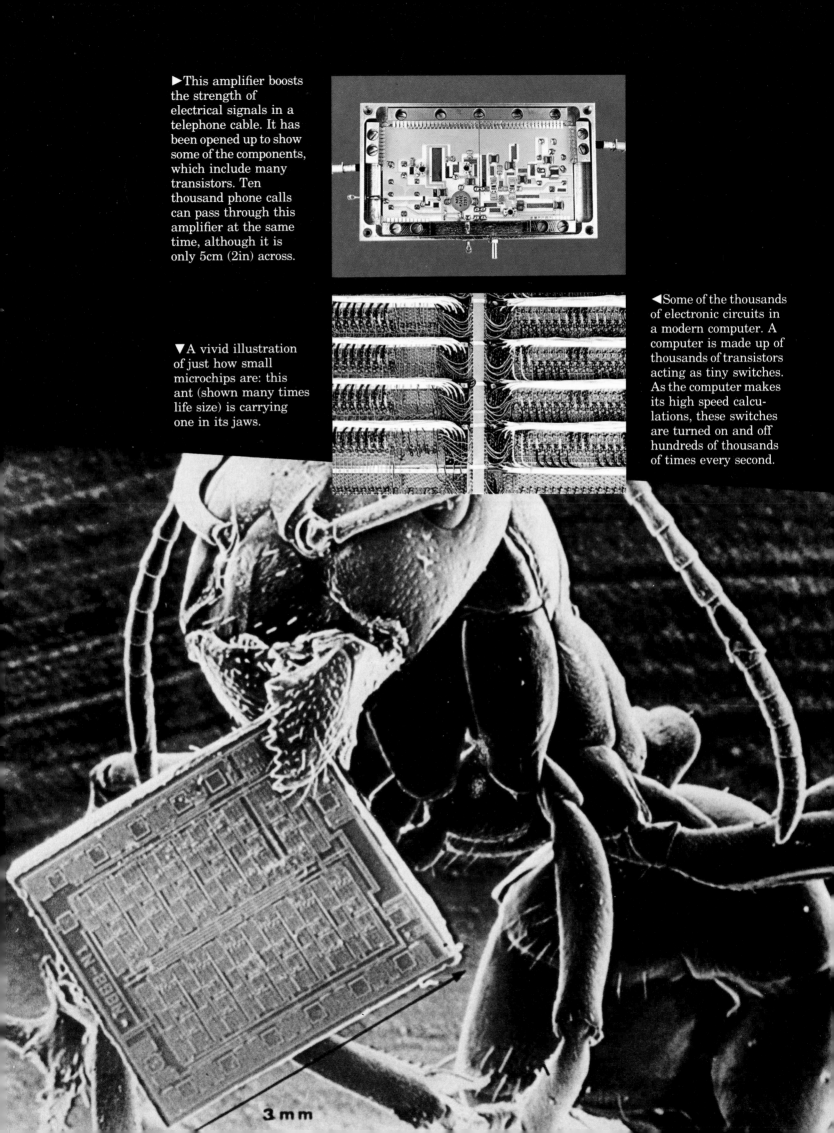

▶This amplifier boosts the strength of electrical signals in a telephone cable. It has been opened up to show some of the components, which include many transistors. Ten thousand phone calls can pass through this amplifier at the same time, although it is only 5cm (2in) across.

▼A vivid illustration of just how small microchips are: this ant (shown many times life size) is carrying one in its jaws.

◀Some of the thousands of electronic circuits in a modern computer. A computer is made up of thousands of transistors acting as tiny switches. As the computer makes its high speed calculations, these switches are turned on and off hundreds of thousands of times every second.

3 mm

p-type semiconductor. If the positive pole of a battery is joined to the p-type semiconductor, and the negative pole is connected to the n-type, a current flows. The battery gives a 'push' to the electrons all round the circuit. The electrons flow into the diode at the n-type side and the electrons already in the n-type semiconductor are pushed on into the p-type material. They continue and leave the diode, flowing round the wire to re-enter the battery.

But if the battery is connected to the diode the other way round, no current will flow. The battery will begin to draw electrons from the n-type side of the diode, but this will leave behind the unbalanced fixed positive charges. Positive and negative charges attract each other strongly, and soon the electrons are held back and cannot flow into the battery. But if electrons are stopped in any part of the circuit, they are stopped everywhere else, too, just as the flow of water cannot be blocked in one part of a hosepipe while continuing normally in the rest of the pipe.

▼Diagrams to show, in a very schematic way, the two types of transistor: the p-n-p transistor and the n-p-n transistor.

A similar thing happens on the p-style side of the diode. Let's think of it in terms of moving positive charges. The charges are drawn out of the diode towards the battery. But the fixed negative charges left behind pull the positive charges so strongly that the flow is brought to a stop.

Diodes are used in your radio. The electric currents from the antenna are alternating – they flow first one way and then the other. They need to be turned into direct – one-way – current. This is done by passing them through diodes.

How transistors work

Now we can look at how a transistor works. It consists of three pieces of semiconductor joined together. In a p-n-p transistor a thin piece of n-type semiconductor is sandwiched between two pieces of p-type material. We shall consider the other kind of transistor, the n-p-n type, which has p-type material between two pieces of n-type material. Both kinds of transistor can be used in the same way.

Suppose the poles of a battery are connected to the two sides of the transistor. The side connected to the negative pole is called the emitter (because it emits, or sends out, electrons that travel through the transistor.) The other piece of n-type material, connected to the positive pole, is called the collector, since it receives those electrons. The p-type semiconductor is called the transistor's base. The transistor is like two diodes joined together. The emitter and base make one of these diodes, and the base and collector make the other.

Current will not yet flow. The collector-base 'diode' has the voltage applied to it the wrong way – the positive pole of the battery is connected to the n-type material. The emitter-base 'diode' *is* connected the right way round – the negative pole to the n-type material – but electrons cannot flow because they cannot cross from the base to the collector.

Now suppose a small positive voltage is applied to the base. This encourages current to flow from the emitter to the base. And the base and collector are now like a diode that has a positive voltage

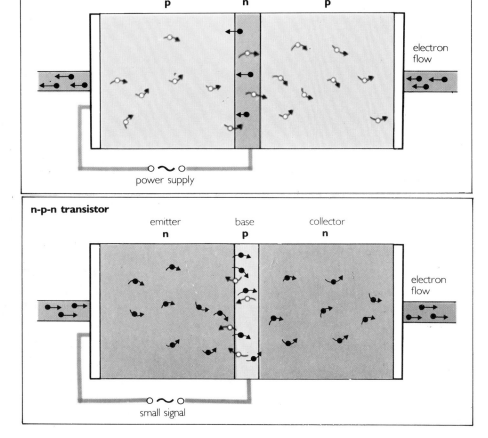

►a An atom of arsenic, which has 33 electrons, five of them in the outer shell. When a few arsenic atoms are included in a germanium crystal as an impurity, **b**, the crystal becomes an n-type semi-conductor – one in which the current consists mainly of electrons. Each arsenic atom has an extra electron compared with the germanium atoms. One electron is easily lost and wanders through the crystal. The arsenic atom is left with a positive charge, **c**. But this atom is fixed, while the negatively charged electrons can wander freely

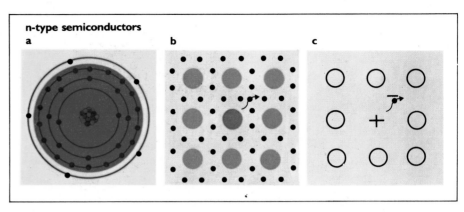

n-type semiconductors
a   b   c

applied to both the p-type and n-type materials. No current flows as a direct result, but the base-collector 'diode' no longer resists the flow of current across it. The electrons from the emitter flow unimpeded across the base, through the collector and out towards the battery.

So the result is that the transistor behaves like a switch. A small positive voltage applied to the base will permit a current – possibly a large one – to flow. Turn off the small base voltage and you block the main current. (Just as a small movement of a mechanical switch can turn a powerful machine on and off.) The transistors used in computers are mostly used in this way, as switches. Thousands of them are formed in *microchips*, which are tiny pieces of semiconducting material.

But in radios transistors are more useful as amplifiers. A small alternating voltage – such as the one from the radio's antenna – is applied to the base. At the same time a large current flows through the transistor. The small voltage is not big enough to switch off the main current, but it will cause it to vary in size. Small variations in the base voltage cause big variations in the main current. But the pattern of the changes, which contains all the necessary information about the words and music in the broadcast, is accurately reproduced in the main current.

Transistors revolutionized electronics when they replaced *valves*. Valves were bulky and used a lot of power. Transistors are small, light and use very little electricity. They made the pocket radio and the portable television set possible. They are also a great deal more reliable than valves.

►a An atom of gallium has 31 electrons, three of them in the outer shell. When added to a germanium crystal, the gallium atoms make a p-type semiconductor. **b** Each gallium atom has one less electron than the germanium atoms. An electron from a nearby atom can easily become attached to the gallium atom, **c** The gallium atom is then negatively charged. A positive charge is left behind near the neighbouring atom, **d** The positive charge can wander through the crystal. So we can think of the electric currents in the crystal as consisting of moving 'positive charges'.

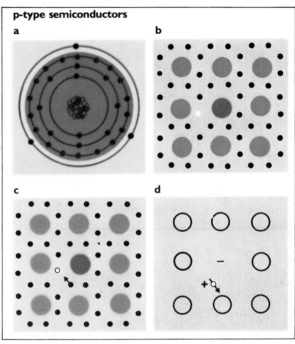

p-type semiconductors
a   b
c   d

►a An atom of germanium, a semiconducting element. There are 32 electrons, all negatively charged. Four are in the outer 'shell'. **b** How the atoms are arranged in a germanium crystal. The atoms 'share' their electrons. **c** Sometimes an electron wanders away from its atom. It leaves behind a positive charge (open circle) where there is a shortage of electrons. **d** If an electric field is applied to the crystal, electrons can move through the crystal. So an electric current flows, which we can think of as made up of electrons moving in one direction and positive charges moving in the other.

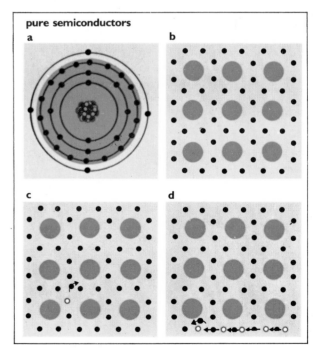

pure semiconductors
a   b
c   d

TELEVISION

▼Television is often used for educational purposes, as well as for entertainment. This set-up is being used by drama students to check how good they are as television actors. They can play back their own performances so that they can watch and correct their faults. This is a closed circuit television system – one in which the TV picture is transmitted along cables to a number of TV sets connected in a circuit. The cameras are remotely controlled. Closed circuit television is frequently used in stores as a security device.

To understand how a TV set receives and displays pictures, we must begin by looking at what happens in the TV camera. First let us look at a black and white camera, the simplest sort.

The TV camera has a lens that focuses light from the scene in front of it. The light is focused to form an image – a picture of the scene – on the 'signal plate' inside the camera. The signal plate is made up of thousands of tiny squares of a special material. When light falls on this material, an electric charge appears at that point. The stronger the light, the larger the electric charge. So there are actually *two* images on the signal plate. There is a visible one, formed by the light from the scene in front of the camera. And there is an invisible electrical 'image', with large electric charges wherever the visible image is bright, smaller charges where the visible image is less bright, and no charge in places where the visible image is dark.

Electrons and electron guns

Now this electrical image has to be turned into a stream of electrical signals – that is, electric currents that carry information about the image. This is done by scanning the signal plate with a beam of *electrons* – tiny electrically charged particles. The beam is fired from a device called an 'electron gun'. The beam sweeps across the plate in horizontal lines, beginning at one corner and finishing in the opposite one. The electrons have 'negative' charge, while the charges on the signal plate are 'positive'. The negative charges cancel out the positive ones, so the beam wipes out the electrical image. It is like washing a freshly painted picture off a wall by sweeping a hosepipe across it from side to side and top to bottom.

But as the charge is removed from each square of the signal plate, a small electric current flows in a wire connected to the plate. The current coming from the plate changes in strength from moment to moment, according to the brightness of

the visible image at the place being scanned by the electron beam.

These electric currents now have to be converted into television waves broadcast from a large antenna (aerial). TV waves are actually UHF (ultra high frequency) radio waves (see page 44). The waves spread out in all directions from the broadcasting antenna. When they reach a home TV antenna, they make electric currents flow in the wire leading to the set. These currents vary in strength in just the same way as the current that came from the signal plate in the camera. Now let's see how they control the way the picture is formed on your TV screen. We are still talking about black and white television only.

At the back of the TV set is an electron gun. The beam of electrons travels forwards and hits the inside of the screen. On the inside of the screen there is a layer of material called a 'phosphor'. This glows briefly whenever electrons strike it.

The electron beam sweeps back and forth across the screen, from left to right and from top to bottom. Its strength varies constantly, according to the strength of the electric currents coming from the aerial. So the screen glows more or less brightly at each spot according to the brightness of the original image in the camera. The TV picture is reproduced accurately – perhaps thousands of miles from the events it shows.

So far we have talked about how a single picture is formed. A series of pictures must be produced rapidly to create the illusion of movement. The signal plate in the camera is scanned many times each second – 25 times in Britain and some other countries, 30 times in the USA. Your TV screen shows the same number of pictures each second.

Colour television

In colour TV, three different pictures are sent. One shows the blue part of the scene, one shows the red part and one shows the green part. These three pictures are enough to build up a picture with all the colours correct – luckily it is not necessary to send a different picture for all the thousands of different shades of colour that we can see.

Inside the colour TV camera light passes through the lens and is then split up into a red, a green and a blue beam by special mirrors. (Each mirror reflects one of these colours and lets the rest through.) Each beam forms an image on a separate signal plate. Suppose the camera is looking at a red apple on a white plate, standing on a tablecloth that has blue and green stripes. In the image formed by the red light, the apple would

▲This was the apparatus used by John Logie Baird, the inventor of television, to transmit the first television picture in 1926. Although the picture was small and flickered badly, research continued successfully – we see the result every time we switch on a TV set.

▼A mobile TV crew can travel to all kinds of outside events. The team may film them or send back 'live' TV pictures to a studio for broadcasting. The man in the centre has a special microphone to pick up sounds and the other two are working the cameras – one mounted on a tripod, the other is handheld and supported on the cameraman's shoulder.

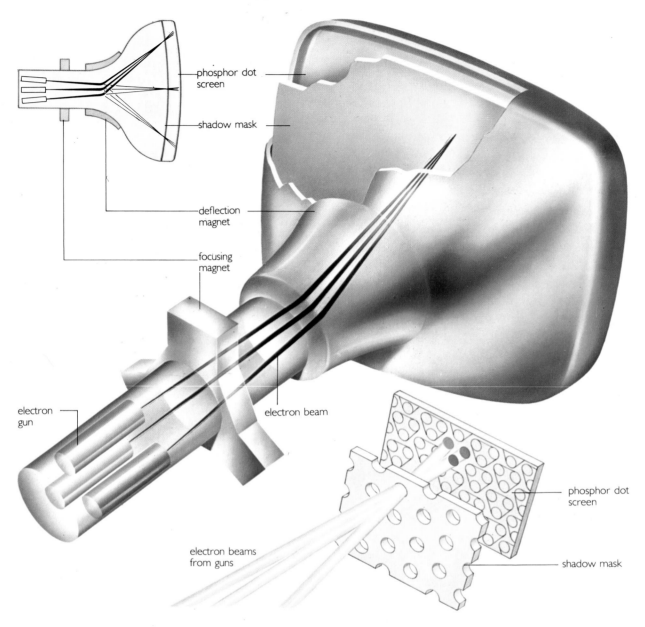

►Diagram showing the working parts of a colour TV tube with its three electron guns and phosphor dot screen. What a contrast to the machine made by Logie Baird less than 60 years ago.

phosphor dot screen

shadow mask

deflection magnet

focusing magnet

electron gun

electron beam

electron beams from guns

phosphor dot screen

shadow mask

show up bright red, while the cloth would be dark, because it doesn't reflect any red light. The plate reflects white light, which is a mixture of all colours. So the plate also looks red in this image. In the green image, the apple looks dark. The green stripes in the tablecloth look bright green, while the blue strips look dark. And the plate also looks green. Can you work out how things look in the image formed by the blue light?

The broadcast TV waves combine all three of these pictures. Your colour TV set has to separate the waves into three parts, and use them to make a red, a green and blue picture. Inside the set there are three electron guns, one for each of these pictures. The back of the screen is coated with thousands of tiny phosphor dots. There are three kinds — one kind glows red when electrons hit it,

another glows green, and the third kind glows blue. There is a 'shadow mask' placed just inside the TV screen. It is a solid sheet of metal with a huge number of tiny holes punched in it. The holes control the three electron beams very accurately. For example, they make sure that the electrons from the gun that makes the red picture hit the red-glowing phosphor dots and not others.

The beams sweep from side to side across the screen. As they 'draw' the red apple, the red phosphor dots glow brightly, because a strong beam of electrons hits them. The green and blue dots do not glow because in that part of the picture, hardly any electrons reach them. But in the part of the picture that shows the white plate, the red, green and blue dots all glow. Our eyes see this mixture of colours as white.

Video

The electric currents that come from the home TV antenna can be recorded on magnetic tape. This is basically just the same process that occurs in sound recording, where the electric currents represent sounds, not pictures (see Tape recorder p. 48). But in a 'video recorder' the tape moves faster than in a sound recorder. When a video recording is played back, it produces electric currents that control the TV set's electron guns in just the same way as the original currents from the receiving antenna.

◀A video-disc playback system works in a similar way to sound records, but plays tapes, not records, and produces a picture and sound.

◀The popularity of video games has been an unexpected spin-off from the introduction of video.

▼Video cassette recorders work on the same principles as audio tape recorders, although the tape is much more complex because it has to record both sound and pictures.

Absolute zero The lowest imaginable temperature, at which all the particles in a body would be completely at rest. It is −273°C (−459°F).

Alternating current An electric current that reverses its direction (alternates) repeatedly. Mains electricity or house current is alternating current (AC).

Amp The unit of electric current. A one-bar electric fire uses a current of about 4 amps.

Amplifier An electronic device that increases (amplifies) the strength of electric currents. Radio and TV sets and record players all use amplifiers.

Anode The part of a battery, valve or other electrical device towards which electrons flow.

Antenna A metal rod or set of rods, or a metal dish, that can detect radio or TV waves. The waves make small electric currents flow in the antenna.

Atom The 'building block' of matter. There are 92 different kinds of naturally occurring atom. They were once thought to be the smallest possible pieces of matter, but we now know they can be broken up into smaller particles.

Boiling point The temperature at which a liquid boils (turns into gas).

Cathode The part of a battery, valve or other electrical device from which electrons flow.

Concave Shaped like the inside of a bowl, with the middle curving away from you.

Conductor A material that allows electric current to pass freely. Metals are good conductors, because electrons can move freely in them.

Convex Shaped like the outside of a bowl, with the middle curving towards you.

Crystal A material in which atoms are arranged in a very orderly pattern – rather like soldiers on parade. A crystal often has a geometrical shape with flat surfaces.

Direct current An electric current that flows in one direction only. The current from a battery is direct current (DC).

Electromagnet A device consisting of many coils of wire through which electric current can flow. While the current is turned on there is a magnetic field. It vanishes when the current is turned off.

Electromagnetic wave A wave consisting of electric and magnetic fields constantly changing in strength. The 'crests' and 'troughs' of the waves are at places where the electric or magnetic fields are strongest. Radio and TV waves, light and X-rays are different kinds of electromagnetic wave.

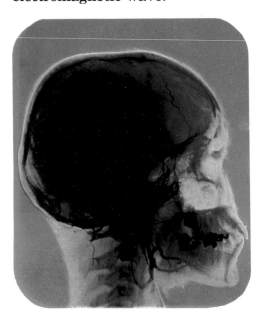

▲X-rays can be used in photography and are very useful in medicine. Can you spot the teeth and vertebrae in these X-ray pictures of the human skull?

Electron One of the particles of which atoms are made. Electrons carry 'negative' electric charge, and an electric current consists of millions of electrons in movement.

Energy When fuel is burned to make a car move, we say that chemical energy stored in the fuel is converted into the car's kinetic energy (energy of movement). When the car stops its kinetic energy is converted into another kind of energy – heat that is generated in the brakes. In a power station heat is converted into electrical energy, which can do all kinds of useful work. Energy appears in all these forms and can be converted from one to the other. It could be described as the ability to make things happen!

Evaporation The gradual turning of a liquid into a vapour (gas). When wet clothes dry out, the water in them evaporates.

Freezing point The temperature below which a liquid turns into a solid. If the solid is warmed it turns into a liquid at the same temperature, so the freezing point is the same as the melting point.

Infra-red radiation Heat radiation – a type of invisible light with wavelength longer than the wavelength of visible light. The infra-red radiation in sunlight can be felt as warmth on the skin.

LCD display The kind of display used on most calculators and digital watches. It uses a thin layer of a 'liquid crystal', which is a little like a crystal and a little like a liquid. When an electric voltage is applied at any place on the liquid crystal that part of it becomes dark. That is how the constantly changing letters and numbers are made. 'LCD' stands for 'liquid crystal diode'.

Microchip A small piece of silicon, often about 6 mm (¼ in) square, on which there are electronic circuits.

▲ This tiny square of silicon, much smaller than the match heads, is a microchip carrying dozens of electronic components.

Photoelectric effect The generation of an electric current in certain materials when light falls on them. Light meters in cameras use the photoelectric effect to measure the brightness of light.

Piezoelectric effect The generation of an electric current in certain crystals when they are squeezed or stretched. When a voltage is applied to the same crystal it contracts (grows smaller) or expands (grows bigger) slightly. Piezoelectric crystals are used in watch and calculator bleepers.

Reflection The 'bouncing back' of light from a surface. We see most objects by the light reflected from their surfaces.

Refraction The bending of a light ray as it passes into or out of a transparent substance. A spoon standing in a glass of water looks distorted because the light reflected from it is refracted as it leaves the water and enters the air.

Stereophonic sound Sound from a record player or tape recorder that seems to be spread out according to the positions of the performers who made the recording. At least two loudspeakers are required to give this effect.

Ultraviolet radiation A type of invisible light with wavelength shorter than the wavelength of visible light. Ultraviolet light in sunshine causes suntan.

Valve In mechanics a valve is a device that allows a fluid such as water or air to pass through in one direction only. In electronics a valve is a device that allows current to flow through it in one direction only.

Voltage Two points are said to be at different voltages if an electric current would flow along a wire joining them. A voltage difference is like a push that makes electrons move.

Wavelength The distance between two crests of a wave – places where the waves are highest or strongest. Ocean waves have wavelengths of many metres; X-rays have wavelengths roughly equal to the distance between atoms in a solid.

INDEX

Acknowledgments
All Sport, BBC Hulton
Picture Library, Paul
Brierley, British Olivetti
Ltd, British Rail,
Capital Radio, Colorific!,
Dunlop Ltd, Ever Ready
Ltd, Richard Francis,
Gilley and Company
Ltd, Halfords Ltd/Metal-
lifacture Ltd, IBM UK
Ltd, Archivio IGDA,
ITN London, The Image
Bank, Kobal Collection,
Lennig Chemicals,
Mansell Collection,
Philips, Picturepoint,
John Pinkerton,
REOSC, Raleigh
Industries, Rex
Features, Science
Museum London, PRO
Audio Department Sony
Broadcast Ltd, Spectrum
Colour Library, Frank
Spooner/Gamma,
Thames Water, Thorn
EMI Ferguson, Richard
Williams Animation
Ltd, ZEFA.